Life as Pilgrimage

Life as Pilgrimage
A View from Celtic Spirituality

David Moffett-Moore, Ph.D.

Cloverdale Books
South Bend

Life as Pilgrimage: A View from Celtic Spirituality

David Moffett-Moore, Ph.D.

Copyright © 2007 by David Moffett-Moore
ALL RIGHTS RESERVED

Cover concept: Becki Moffett-Moore

Published by
Cloverdale Books
An Imprint of Cloverdale Corporation
South Bend, Indiana 46601

www.CloverdaleBooks.com

Library of Congress Cataloging-in-Publication Data

Moffett-Moore, David.
  Life as pilgrimage : a view from Celtic spirituality / David Moffett-Moore.
      p. cm.
  Summary: "Using the Peregrine falcon as an archetype for pilgrimage, this
volume explores the roots of our ancient past to discover meaning for our
modern lives. Celtic pilgrimage is about the journey rather than the
destination: life is a pilgrimage from the place of our birthing to the place of
our rising"--Provided by publisher.
  Includes bibliographical references.
  ISBN-13: 978-1-929569-35-9 (pbk.)
  ISBN-10: 1-929569-35-1 (pbk.)
  1. Christian pilgrims and pilgramages. 2. Spirituality--Celtic Church.
  3. Falcons. 4. Birds--Religious aspects--Christianity. I. Title.

  BV5067.M64 2007
  248.089'916--dc22

                                    2007015824

Printed in the United States of America
on recycled paper made from 100% post-consumer waste

Contents

To my parents, John and Ruth, who gave me roots,
And my wife, Becki, who gives me wings,
And all my fellow Pilgrims,
Who grace me with Holy Company.

Prologue

A lone falcon soars high overhead, its fleeting shadow invisible amongst the tall prairie grass, wafting in the wind. With eyes as piercing as they appear, it surveys its surroundings for some unsuspecting prey. Targeting a young pheasant in flight, the falcon begins its stoop: a steep dive sometimes in excess of 200 miles per hour. The unsuspecting pheasant never knows its own death is so near. The falcon strikes with its claw outstretched as it descends upon its prey, slashing the pheasant's throat. After the strike, the falcon circles back, catching the now dying pheasant in its own descent, and carries it off for its feast. The entire attack lasts less than sixty seconds. It is the cycle of life: something lives and something dies and something continues to live.(1)

A falcon in flight is a thing of wonder and beauty, filled with power and grace. Too often it goes unnoticed in our daily lives. Falcons were worshiped as gods by the ancient Egyptians and prized by nobility in the Middle Ages. Smaller than eagles, buzzards or vultures, they excel them all as hunters.

"Peregrine" comes from the Latin for pilgrim, or wanderer, a name that aptly applies to the peregrine falcon. They are birds in constant flight, known to migrate as far as 10,000 miles, farther than any other bird, living lives of constant pilgrimage, as their name implies. Pilgrims in flight, they no sooner arrive than it is time for their departure. Their lives are defined by their flight: they are pilgrims, and so long as they live, they are on pilgrimage.

Like the falcon we have named, we too are peregrines, pilgrims, travelling through the journey of our life. Like the Peregrine, we are born for the flight, for the journey. Like the Peregrine, we are born for the hunt. Our flight is the journey of our lives; our hunt is the search for meaning to our existence. We are born for this hunt, this quest, and our lives are restless without it. It is the search for our own soul, the soul of our existence. We may ignore this instinctual desire, but it is to our peril. We substitute other desires, but this unmet hunger still compels us. We can build a society that is blind to it, as a barrier against it, but our quest for meaning will find a way through.

We live in a very fast paced, outwardly focused, materially minded world that seems to be on a single minded pursuit of immediate personal physical gratification, a consumerist society that is eager, even anxious, to acquire and possess absolutely everything possible. We live in a world that has lost its soul.

Our society has grown increasingly secular and material. There is little sense of the sacred and only a limited sense of the spiritual. The only reality that is acknowledged is a physical reality. Those who do express spiritual longings typically distinguish themselves and their spirituality from institutionalized religion, of any tradition.

Yet the search for personal meaning is as much a part of human existence as is the search for the physical necessities of life. A sense of meaning and purpose is as important to our well being as is food, shelter and clothing. We have an innate, even genetic, desire to see meaning, purpose and structure in our lives and have been known to create it out of our own imagination where it does not otherwise independently exist. We ignore this inner longing not only to our peril, but to the detriment of civilization itself.

We have taken personal independence to the extreme of psychotic narcissism. Society has grown increasingly splintered and fractured, even atomized, into a cacophony of personal interest groups, each more obsessed with not allowing others to succeed than in finding their own fulfillment. It becomes more important that others lose than it is that we win. We have turned wants to needs and luxuries to necessities, and in our greed not realized that there is never "enough" if our hearts are empty. We have turned perseverance into impatience and created road rage and in our greed, forced bankruptcies. Not only is there a deterioration of civilization, there is a loss of civility.

Yet the humans who have gone before us have acknowledged a non-physical element to our life that is just as essential for our well-being as are food, shelter and clothing. Late in his career, Sigmund Freud was asked in an interview what was necessary for human emotional health. His answer was, "Love and work." (2) A sense of purpose and a sense of caring. Physicians and psychologists have long agreed on the individuals need to love and to be loved. This is true physically as well as emotionally; our immune system is stronger if we are in caring relationships with others. Neither a sense of caring nor a sense of purpose are physical manifestations; neither are tangible entities. Yet both are essential for our long term health.

We need to find a way out, or perhaps remember a way in, a way to rediscover our own personal soul and together, our collective soul.

In the ancient world, primitive humans and society experienced awe and wonder in their everyday lives; they felt the presence of mystery around them and within. They held life as a sacred event and the world as a beautiful gift. It was a thing to be enjoyed rather than consumed, to be in relationship with rather than to be possessed. Among the ancients, the Celtic Christians especially preserved this ancient wisdom and found a way to mingle it with their newfound Christian faith, thus creating a special expression for their spiritual experience of life, a metamorphosis of the ancient and the modern, a unique approach to living in their time and place, that has a message that can help us in our own time and place.

The Celtic Christians believed and experienced life as a holy festival, meant to be enjoyed fully, cherished lovingly and shared generously. They knew life to be a pilgrimage. Not a pilgrimage according to Roman or Western tradition, nor Eastern nor modern secular versions, all of which view pilgrimage as a journey focused on the destination. For these traditions, the point is to reach the destination, after which the pilgrimage is over. Celtic pilgrimage is about the journey, not the destination. "Life is a journey from the place of our birthing to the place of our rising." (3) Our goal is not to reach the destination as quickly and easily as possible, but rather to enjoy the journey, to experience the fullness of our traveling along the way. Life is about the journey, and our meaning is found in experiencing fully the opportunities that lie before us along the way. If life is a pilgrimage, then our lives are meant to stay on the way, for when our pilgrimage ends we are no longer pilgrims.

The purpose of this book is to invite the reader to live a more aware life, a life lived more fully in the present moment, a life that is more fully conscious of itself and of its surroundings, and therefore may truly be enjoyed because it is more fully known and experienced. This life is described as part of the primitive experience and part of the human experience. It is expressed most fully within the Celtic tradition.

Human spirituality is about the sense of meaning and purpose in one's life and about the awareness of the experience of life. This is the meaning of human consciousness, the essence of who we are. It is a sense of being in relationship, with one's self, with others, both human and with all of life, and with the ultimate other, the whole of life, the one we call God. Human spirituality is to experience life as holy and a gift to be loved rather than a thing to be used.

The quest of the pilgrimage has been a part of every civilization as an expression of our longing for that which is more, that which is beyond us. The Celtic Christians made this a part of their daily lives and we can learn this approach from them. The symbol for this sense of life as a pilgrimage is found in the bird that bears the name, the Peregrine falcon, "the Pilgrim."

Acknowledgements

"Life is a pilgrimage, from the place of our birthing to the place of our rising." So say our Celtic forebearers, making each day a holy day, each place a holy place, each person a fellow pilgrim, and all life a sacred festival. And giving us much to be thankful for.

For parents, who surround us with love and fill us with courage, saying, "David, you can be anything you want to be, you can do anything you set out to do." For family, who love us no matter what, in spite of all the things that make us distinctly ourselves. For teachers, who fill our minds with ideas and our hearts with dreams, who give us opportunity to try our wings where it is safe to fail, and encourage us to try again. For friends, whose company doubles our joys and halves our sorrows. For strangers met along the way, whose accidental passings have serendipitous results. For the hurts and brokenness, the failures and sorrows, without which life would not be complete, without which the joys and successes would not be as precious. For all things, I acknowledge my gratefulness and give thanks.

For Mrs. Knote's fourth grade class assignment, asking us to write about what we wanted to be when we grew up. My answer was not a cowboy, fireman or astronaut. I wanted to have a Ph.D. and a book published in my name. For the staff, faculty and community of Graduate Theological Foundation, that provided the means forty five years later to make the life dream of a ten year old come true.

For all the churches I've served over the years, communities of faith and love that held me in grace and filled me with hope, that helped me find ways to be true to myself, to continue my search, and give me opportunity to serve someone besides myself and be part of something truly big.

For the people and programs of Lindenwood Retreat and Conference Center, part of my life and pilgrimage these past twenty five years, where I have studied and prayed and served and led. Truly a "thin place" if ever there was one.

For Dick Stegner at Garrett-Evangelical, Irv Batdorf at United and Warren Adams at Earlham, all professors who stretched my thoughts and challenged me to grow while taking me as I was. Especially for Earlham College, which taught me to truly think. For Marlene Kropf, of Associated Mennonite Biblical Seminary, who as faculty at Graduate Theological Foundation served as my Ordinarius through the dissertation process and worked with me at Lindenwood. Marlene's grace and wisdom both taught and comforted me along the way.

For all those who have gone the way before me, those who wrote the books I have read and shared their stories, especially for all the nameless ones, those who have walked their ways in silence and kept alive a sometimes flickering flame illuminating the wonder of this world. And for the readers, who in this book now hold the baton and in their turn, pass it on to future generations who will make the pilgrimage of life, and by whose passing will make it holy.

Flight of the Falcon

The falcon is born for the flight and born to hunt. Its flight requires a great deal of energy, so it is always vigilant for the opportunity to replenish its reserves. It is both at one with its environment and fully aware of its environment, qualities that in humans we would call consciousness. Beautiful on the wing and an acrobatic flyer, the falcon exhibits strength that exceeds its size.

The falcon has a voracious appetite and is a vigilant hunter. Gorging on as much as it can eat, the bird also packs its crops, the pouches in its neck, to carry additional food. The falcon is one of the most aggressive hunters in the animal world. It will only rest a short while before continuing its flight.

The mighty eagle does not live up to its publicity. It is easily satisfied by feeding on carrion and is known to steal the catch from other birds of prey. Benjamin Franklin protested its use as a national symbol, arguing that it was tainted by its use among the European monarchies and that the United States would not feed upon the carcasses of others or plunder the wealth of other nations. His recommendation was a bird native to the Americas, the wild turkey. But the falcon also does not steal or devour the catch of others.

The Egyptians honored their god Horus as the sun god, ruler of the heavens. With the head of a hawk, it was the son of Osiris, ruler of the afterlife and judge of the dead, and Isis, goddess of fertility and of life. It is fitting that the falcon, which rules the skies, would be so honored by the ancients as a deity and a sign of the divine.

Medieval society had strict regulations about who could own which type of falcon. The birds were respected as having a dignity and a hierarchy of their own, and this was reflected in the human rules of ownership. The merlin, the smallest of the falcons, could be owned by the gentry. The peregrine, slightly larger than the merlin, could be owned by the nobility. The gyrfalcon, the largest of these hunting birds and therefore the ruler of the falcons, could only be owned by those of royal blood. Of the three, it was the peregrine that was most noted for its boldness and tenacity, taking on birds two and three times its own size and willing to fight almost from the time of its hatching and to its own dying. (4)

As with most birds of prey, the female is larger than the male. Female peregrines typically measure 20 inches and weigh 30 ounces. Males are about 15 inches and 18 ounces and are called "tiercels" - from the French word for "third," being about one third less the size of the female.(5) They contain a lot of fight for a bird, weighing barely a pound. Today it is the Peregrine that is most prized by falconers as a hunting bird, known to be fierce and unafraid. Its defiant gaze makes it appear always ready for the hunt, for the fight.

About the same size as a crow, but stronger and more agile, peregrines have a unique silhouette, with a short neck, long pointed wings and a short narrow tail. They have a slate grey back and a barred white belly; their head looks like a black helmet with sideburns. They hunt from dawn to dusk because they need to consume their own weight in food.

2

They are incredibly agile in flight and are known to practice their moves in feigned aerial battles with one another. They have exceptional hearing and eyesight and their bodies are built for speed. They will stay aloft for hours, can maintain standard flight in excess of 60 miles an hour and their stoops, or dives, will exceed 200 miles an hour, making them by far the fastest animal alive. Even in their genetic design, falcons have been bred for their destiny. Their skulls contain special cavities to help them withstand the pressures of such speed. With their sharp talons and crooked beak they are fierce predators, and with their strong feet they are capable of carrying kills many times their own weight. Noted for possessing perfect aim, their eyes are capable of reading the words on this page from a mile away. They are identified by their mustache markings under their eyes, that serve much the same purpose as the black stripe worn on the cheeks of athletes: to reduce glare and improve their vision.

Peregrines mate for life and typically keep the same nest, or eyrie, to raise their young. Their chicks are called "eyas" and are ready to fly at six weeks. Certainly possessing the instincts of a hunter, the parents still teach their young and help them hone their skills both for flight and for finding food. They are born to be pilgrims, wanderers; designed for flight and destined to spend their lives wandering the world - always traveling, never arriving. They end one season's migration only to begin another one, not so much stopping as resting. From their birthing to their dying, their life is one of constant pilgrimage

In the 1950's and 1960's they became nearly extinct, due to the use of dichloro-diphenyl-trichloroethane, commonly known as ddt, and other pesticides. The

3

poisons were ingested by the birds and other animals upon which the Peregrines preyed, and then these chemicals became concentrated within the Peregrines' systems. We and all creatures are part of the web of life and not independent of it. Whatever we do to the web, we do to ourselves. While not particularly detrimental to the victim, the pesticides resulted in critically weakened shells for their young. Weaker shells meant fewer survivors, and those that did survive were themselves weaker. The struggle to get free from the shell served to strengthen the young and better prepare them for the rigors of their own existence. When this was realized, ddt was banned by the Environmental Protection Agency, and efforts were made to help the species survive. Eggs were surreptitiously taken from eyries so that they could be incubated and the eyas could be nursed and released into the wild. With this help, the species seems confident of survival.(6)

Life is a good thing. In all its trials and confusions, life remains a good thing and a gift to be cherished, in all its variety and diversity; all the forms, shapes and expression life takes. Cosmologists postulate that from its beginning, the universe has been striving for the creation of life, and particularly life that can be aware of its own existence and understand its experience. We are a life form that can experience and understand, can gain awareness of its existence. This desire to understand what we experience, to know why we exist, is a part of our nature. It is our quest and our destiny, our yearning. Indeed, the search for meaning is the reason for our existence; not just the meaning or finding the meaning, but the search itself. We are born for the quest, the

4

pilgrimage. The Peregrine falcon is an appropriate symbol of this urge in our life.

The Peregrine falcon is aptly named, for it is a perpetual pilgrim. Beginning life in a nest as a nursling crying out to be fed, to be nurtured and nourished, it learns to fly and hunt while yet quite young and sets off immediately on its own. Barely months old, the Peregrine begins its first migration to warmer climes, hunting while it is flying, resting only to eat and sleep. On some days it will cover over a thousand miles, flying almost constantly. At the end of their fall migration, they rest only a while and do not really stop, for they no sooner arrive than they prepare for their return to the place of their origin, their true home. They rest, they eat, they restore their strength and what scant reserves their aerodynamic frames allow.

Then it all begins again. They fly, they soar, they stalk, they stoop. They eat and rest and fly again. Their flights are wonders of nature: sixty miles an hour in flight, 200 miles an hour when diving, a thousand miles some days, ten thousand miles in all. In a pilgrimage that has been their life, they arrive at the place of their beginning and know it for the first time. Mating, they build an eyrie, raise their eyas, only to fly again. Always the flight is before them, always the journey beckons them, they live ever the pilgrim, ever the wanderer.

Like our mobile society, the Peregrine is always on the move, but unlike so much in our society, the Peregrine moves with meaning. It always stays in touch with the reality around it, aware of its surroundings. The Peregrine has an intensity in its gaze, a vigilance in its stance. It lives on the alert. It is not simply passing through, it is living fully in each moment. A pilgrim is not a tourist, out

5

to see the sights. A pilgrim is on an outer journey with an inner purpose. The Peregrine is the pilgrim of birds, and as such serves as an apt symbol for our own journey toward meaning.

The Peregrine is a beautiful bird and magnificent in its flight. A thing of wildness and a creature of wonder, it must survive many dangers to maintain its own existence, and that of its species. Fierce and free, it is a bird born to be constantly in flight, always restless, ever wandering, eternally the pilgrim for which it is named.

Like the Peregrine, we are destined to be pilgrims, on the journey, wandering and wondering. Life is a pilgrimage from the place of our birthing to the place of our rising again.

Original Paradise

Primitive humans were very much like the modern Peregrine. They were at one with their surroundings, in touch with the world that so much touched them. They were fully aware of the immediacy of their experiences, fully present in the present moment. Their world was filled with awe and wonder, and their lives were filled with mystery and magic. They lived with a sense of immanent transcendence, that all life was sacred and every moment divine.

This is a time before time, before history and civilization, before calendars and clocks, before schedules and appointments, before ipods and palm pilots. Time was "the eternal now." The world was "all I see from horizon to horizon." If I close my eyes, it all ceases to be; when I open them, they all return to me again.

Victor Turner writes about the primitive experience in his classic, The Ritual Process,(7) describing the sense of divine presence with which everyday life is approached. During the 1950's, Turner lived among the Ndembu, an aboriginal tribe in Africa, and studied their experience of our world as primitives. They lived in the same world, on the same planet, as moderns, yet their experience of it was entirely different. The primitive consciousness is not the same as the modern consciousness, even though our bodies are the same. We are genetically identical, but psychologically different. We may have the same experiences, but we will experience them differently.

Turner describes their life as a "liminal" experience: life lived on the threshold, life lived "in process". The ritualizing of life is a way to recognize life's ultimacy, life's meaning. Imbuing everyday experiences with a sense of ritual is a way both to recognize and to experience the sacredness of life, of existence, in and through everyday events.

This difference in awareness, difference in consciousness, is a notable distinction separating the primitive peoples of the world from the modern people. We are on the same planet at the same time, we may have the same experiences, but we will experience them differently. It is not the "what" that is different: the objective experiences may be the same. It is the "why" that is different: our sense of the world within which we live and of ourselves within that world is different. For the primitives all presence is divine presence, all time is holy and all space is sacred. This sense of Divine Presence, of Cosmic Consciousness, of the Holy Other, of the "that which is more," is something that defines the primitive approach to life. All primitive people, of all time and in all places, have possessed it. Modern people do not. Yet we live in the same world.

Modern people tend to think of primitives as being superstitious in this belief in a divine presence, a cosmic consciousness. Yet quantum science tells us that the cosmos does have an awareness, even a consciousness. Experiments identify that the objects within the experiment respond to the human object observing the experiment, that the results we find can be predicted by the way we search, and we are more subjects in relationship than objects observing and being observed. The primitive consciousness and the mystical language of the world's religions come closer to agreeing with the view of quantum science than does the paradigm of cold rationality.(8)

Among primitive people, all life is experienced as holy, as sacred time and space, and existence itself is divine. The Almighty Eternal is completely immanent, filling all creation with being itself and causing all things to be. The Almighty Eternal is absolute other, so above and beyond all experience and expression that it can only be guessed at, hunches from a mind dark with mystery like a hand groping in a darkened room, where one may feel but not fully know what is felt. Imagination fills the gaps left in the experiences that cannot be explained with stories meant to be expressive rather than definitive, meant to inspire rather than explain, so that the hearer may also share in the experience.

Life is a life of pilgrimage, a life lived "on the way" and as a journey. We see this in the example of the primitive human societies still on our planet: the aborigines of Africa, Australia and Indonesia; the Inuit of the Arctic; the remote tribes along the Amazon. Few they be and far between, and each threatened by modernity, yet they stand as living reminders of the seed from which all civilization has grown. They remind us of who we are and where we are from.

Humans lived in small tribes of extended families, enough in number so that they could survive, few enough so that they could know and be known by one another. Each day was spent seeking food for survival that day: scattering in the morning to hunt, whether for game or for fruit and nuts and berries; gathering that night to share the wealth that had been claimed with others, so that all had enough and none had too much; moving as a clan in migration with the birds of the air and the animals of the field in their own migrations, so that life mimics life and life is one with life.

As the mysteries of life are realized, hunter-gatherers slowly developed into farmer-settlers. The ways of fruits, vegetables and grains are discovered and, with them, a more stable and secure, less strenuous and tenuous lifestyle is achieved. Still, human life was at one with the natural world, and the natural world is filled with divine mystery and wonder. Human cultivation and development, the exploitation of our surroundings, led to a super-abundance, to producing more than we can consume and making more than we can use. Wealth was defined by things possessed rather than people known and experiences shared. Families became tribes, tribes became clans, clans became societies, societies became civilizations. The quest for life to maintain one's existence became the quest for power to vainly prove one's superiority over another.

This is not the view of society originated by English philosopher Thomas Hobbes in <u>Leviathon</u>, with the social contract holding our society together and based upon cooperative self-interest, without which life is "solitary, short, mean and brutish" without some subliminal social contract.(9) Nor is it the romanticized view of Jean Jacque Rousseau of the French Enlightenment, of humans in their native state living as "noble savages," their pride, self-preservation and reason leading them to form natural friendships with others and their world. His view was that civilization corrupted the natural discourse of humans, filling them instead with jealousy, fear and suspicion.(10) It is simply life, human life in the midst of a living world, with all its expressions and permutations. Neither ideal nor savage, it just is.

Whatever else life is, it is real. And it is all that we have. We may as well make the best of it! Life is that which is within us, quickening us. Life is all that is around us. Not just the animals that live and breathe, that breed and die, but the plants as well, that burst from their seeds, grow and flourish and promulgate their seed after them. Life is also the rock beneath our feet, heaving up as mountains, breaking into boulders, splintering into gravel and deteriorating still further to become the soil beneath our feet, giving sustenance to the plants that nourish the animals that decay to fertilize the earth that gives us life. Life is the cloud in the sky, watering the earth, irrigating the field and eroding the mountain, running to the sea in brooks and rivers that themselves support grasses and insects and fish before evaporating in the oceans to form clouds again. Life is all and in all. Life is a cycle, constantly changing and growing, constantly renewing and restoring itself. Life is the dynamic tension between birth and death, between prey and predator, where each one takes its turn and serves its purpose. Life is the whole and life is the balance. And all of it, all of it, is right and proper and due its honor.

In the Bible, the prophets declare, "the earth will be filled with the knowledge of the glory of God, even as the waters cover the sea."(Isaiah 11:9, Habakkuk 2:14)

This is the world as the primitives saw it, and the primitives among us see it still. It is the way we see it when we are young. When we are young we are all primitives living in a mystical world. When we are young, all life is filled with awe and wonder and each day a living miracle. Our constant reaction is "Wow!" It is a

11

magical world with treasures everywhere and we live in awe and wonder. Life is a mystery and every child a mystic. As children, we are always fully present in the present moment, fully alive in a world that is alive, fully aware of our experience. Life has an immediacy and an urgency to it, and each moment of every day is lived to the full. A child rests easily at night, its energy spent in living fully the day, its conscience clear of any regrets or wrongs, its dreams filled with the hope and possibility of still better days yet ahead.

Remember those days? Remember being young enough, free enough, to be fully present in the present moment, to live each day for all its worth, to experience the wonder and excitement that came with each passing moment? Remember the stillness of watching a butterfly in flight, a flower in bloom, or waiting for the grass to grow? And over each hill was another world waiting to be discovered. When we were young, we were as primitives. The world was alive and we were aware, our imaginations alive with the glory that was always all around us, even within us.

We were as Peregrines on the wing, soaring high and watching it all. Swooping down upon the least little thing with all our awareness, we approached life with our whole being. We flew, we dove, we wandered. We never settled; we only rested, for there was always another adventure to be lived, another experience to explore. We were Peregrines with eyes absorbing it all, Peregrines that floated among the clouds, Peregrines that grabbed life like a prey in our claws, Peregrines that were always ready for the next moment, the next move, always ready for the journey of experience and awareness we now call life.

When we were children, we knew the secret. All life is holy festival, meant to be lived fully, shared generously, experienced completely, cherished lovingly, and to be let go of graciously when our own time comes. When we were children, we were as Peregrines. How did we forget?

Civilization and Its Discontents

As primitives, we were at one with the world, we lived in and as one with the others in our tribe. We were at one with the world, at one with the One in our experience of the divine presence and at one with the All in our sense of unity with all creation, wholly present to the wholly Other.

As hunter-gatherers, we experienced life as a garden paradise, where all we wanted was within our grasp and all people shared in the bounty of an abundant creation. Life was lived in the balance, in the flow between the one and the all, between scattering for the hunt and gathering for the celebration.

As farmer-settlers, we gained a greater security and stability in our existence, but the gain always comes with a loss. We gave up a bit of our freedom in giving up our wandering. We became less a part of the world we lived in and more an object distinct from it. In Thomas Berry's phrase, we were less a "community of subjects" and more a "collection of objects."(11) Seeking a dependability from nature meant forcing our control upon it.

Certainly, civilization meant definite improvements in our quality of life and gave us the luxury of producing more than we could use. But storing our abundance became hoarding our wealth. We had time that we had not had before. Instead of spending all our time hunting and gathering or in farming, we had time for creativity and personal expression, for arts and culture. Early civilizations still recognized the sacredness of life and spent much of their available free time honoring that sacredness through ritual expression, something we came to see as "religion."

Early civilizations in India, China, Egypt, Iraq and the Americas all share the same basic concepts: a sense of community in walled cities, separating that which is "of us" from that which is not; erecting bins to store excess wealth; building palaces to house those who had come to dominate, to rule over their compatriots as subjects; and establishing areas for worship and sacrifice, which typically were the centers of the community.

Something was gained. Life was more stable, the world seemed more dependable. Something was lost. Quest for power had risen and there was less struggle to survive. As civilizations grew, more people lost freedom and equality. Still, there remained the sense of the sacred that had always been a part of the human experience of existence on this planet. Life had a sense of purpose and meaning. We may not have always known what the reason for it all was, but we knew that there was a reason.

With the gain of civilization, there was another loss, unrecognized. A more settled life meant no more wandering. No more hunting and gathering meant we were not roaming the world, we became less "at one" and "as one" with it. No wandering physically also meant no wandering spiritually. When we became farmer-settlers, we ceased being pilgrim-wanderers. We ceased being peregrines. This loss meant a wounding of our soul. We gained civilization, but it came at great cost.

We lost our sense of relationship with the world around us, our sense of being at one with our environment. We lost our sense of wonder in the world around us, and with it, we lost the sense of joy at simply being alive. In losing our relationship with the world around us, we even lost a part of our own sense of self, our true self, and began to accumulate a false sense of self. When we stopped being pilgrims, we stopped being ourselves. A pilgrim always has a sense of purpose and of direction. A pilgrim knows who he or she is and where she or he is going. How many times have we found ourselves wondering about our purpose in life, about the meaning of our existence, about the direction of our lives?

In his book, <u>Civilization and its Discontents</u>, Sigmund Freud analyzes this cost-benefit of society.(12) The gain in civilization comes at a loss to the individual: a loss of freedom, of both expression and of experience. Each individual must give up something of themselves to become a part of the civilization. In terms of Utilitarian philosophy, most fully expressed by the English philosopher John Stuart Mill, there is a dynamic tension between the needs of the many and the needs of the one, and the one is always outvoted. Utilitarianism pronounces morally good any act that adds to the happiness of society as a whole.(13) A contented civilization, then, means by necessity there will be discontented individuals. It can be no other way. The benefits gained by the development of civilization carry with them a loss within the person.

Part of Freud's argument was against the influence of religion, as something used to control and manipulate the masses, "the opiate of the masses,"(14) yet every civilization has had its religion. It has been argued that to be human means, at least in part, to be religious; it is

17

impossible to be human without also being religious. There is both religious expression in ritual and symbol and religious institutions that provide structure, emotionally and physically, for this religious expression.

By way of contrast, Mircea Eliade argues in The Sacred and the Profane that finding the sacred in space, time and nature is part of the very core of our humanity and that moderns claiming to live in a profane world are still fed by a sense of the sacred, however unconscious and disintegrated it may be. (15)

In The Mystic Heart, Wayne Teasdale lifts up a universal mysticism behind the spiritual traditions of each of the world's religions. (16) He traces the development of institutional religion from its seminal mystic experience, and roots out that original mysticism beneath the layers of religious structure, identifying their common elements.

The sense of being "at one with the One" or "at one with the All," of being a part of the whole of life rather than apart from it, is the classic mystical experience. Every religion begins with this. The mystical experience is a part of the human experience. People who have profound personal mystical experiences are seen as spiritual leaders, and they develop a following. Spiritual traditions develop that are designed to help practitioners to attain these mystical experiences. Eventually, religious institutions are constructed to house and support these spiritual traditions. Sometimes within a few generations, we have moved from mystical experiences that are part of the human experience and enable us to feel whole, to religious institutions that frequently inhibit the very experiences they were originally designed to nurture. This process is repeated in every religion, and every religion has at its heart the mystical experience.

We can see this in the historical development of Christianity. Jesus of Nazareth is the founder of the faith, living approximately from 6 B.C.E. to 30 C.E. His followers endeavored to keep alive the faith of Jesus, yet within a generation, faith in Jesus rather than the faith of Jesus, seems to have prevailed. This may be clearly seen in the writing of the apostle Paul, comprising nearly half the New Testament. By the end of the first century, the structures of the religion of Christianity are coming into place and by the Nicene Council in the fourth century, the transformation is complete. Christianity had moved from the mystical experience of its founder to the spiritual traditions of his followers and then the religious institutions of the next generation.

The central theme of Freud's book is that the benefits of civilization come at a cost to the individual. Marx makes the same argument in his classic, <u>Das Kapital</u>, though from an economic perspective rather than a psychological one. In his explanation, property owners take advantage of laborers. This is a reverse of Utilitarianism, with the few taking advantage of the many.(17) In any case, there are clear and strong arguments that the gains of civilization have come at a loss to the individual.

Modern western civilization has exacted an especially severe cost upon the individual. Our particular version of civilization is one driven by material consumption. It is not enough to produce more than we can consume, we must consume even more, and then produce more. This only creates a vicious cycle we call economic growth. It

19

may benefit economic indicators, but at the loss of our humanity.

It is not enough to accumulate greater abundance, we must hoard all that we can accumulate. If our houses aren't big enough, we must build bigger houses. If our cars aren't large enough, we must build larger vehicles. If we can't contain all we possess, we must rent additional storage units. The entire focus of our lives becomes to accumulate and consume ever increasing amounts of exclusively material things. Those parts of our lives that are not tangible, that can't be consumed or acquired, have no value: our relationships, our friendship, our marriages, our psyche, our soul, our spirituality.

As the saying goes, if you win the rat race, you're still a rat.

As our modern lives continue to focus exclusively on the outward, physical life, our inner spiritual life has suffered much. This unconscious loss has led to an ever increasing source of stress, tension and personal conflict. We possess more, but we become less: less happy, less content, less confident, less fulfilled, even less human.

We are as Peregrines who only hunt and eat, pilgrims who have lost their way and are sated by their consumption. They've forgotten to fly; they've forgotten that they were born not for the hunt but for the flight, not merely to consume but for the quest. Pilgrims who have left the pilgrimage cannot be true to their own nature. Instead, their confusion will grow to frustration and frustration to rage, lost within themselves.

Self as Serf, Society as Lord

Western civilization experienced a grand flowering during the classical age of the Greeks and Romans. The West was united in common speech and government. Travel and trade was possible between East and West, making for an almost global community the like of which would not be experienced again for another 1500 years. The collapse of the Roman Empire in the West, in the face of the massive migrations of the Germanic tribes, meant the loss of common government and of common language. The rise of Islam served as a barrier between East and West. Civilization itself seemed to be a grand experiment that now was doomed to fail.

The rise of Medieval society created a much more insularly, inwardly focused society that spent all of its energy in maintaining the status quo, stability and constancy at all costs. This meant, of course, little progress. Change is not always progress, but progress is always change, and Medieval society feared change.

The rise of Medieval society also led to the development of serfdom. Unless of noble birth, the individual was of no value. Common folk became the possession of the land they tilled and the soil they worked. They were not slaves, in that they were not owned by another person. They belonged to the land, but not in the sense that the primitives did.(18)

Primitives were at one with the land and at one with their environment, a part of rather than apart from. There was not a sense of ownership, just a sense of awareness and identity. Serfs were not at one with the land or at one with their environment. They worked the land; they were objects in their environment, not subjects of it. The environment was an object to them, a thing to be used, tilled and harvested, but not a subject with which to interact or relate. Yet serfs were tied to the land, in a sense owned by the land. They were not free to leave it, free to wander and roam. As monks would take vows of chastity, poverty and stability, so serfs effectively had a vow of stability. They had to stay in the village where they were born.

There was a loss of the individual, a loss of imagination, a loss of spirit to go with the loss of soul and loss of self. The individual was lost to the society, the soul was lost as the mystical experience in everyday life gave way to rising superstition. Imagination was lost to the aggressive determination to maintain the status quo. And the self was lost to itself; there was no sense of self. The serfs belonged to their village and their land. Even the king was owned by the land; the Medieval concept was that the land and the king were one. As one thrived, the other thrived; when the king grew weak, the land suffered.

Classical civilization supported commerce between East and West and allowed individual travel. It may not have been entirely safe, but it certainly was possible and generally permitted. By contrast, medieval civilization was insular and isolated. There existed only fanciful tales of foreign lands and people, both noble and serf, were tied to the land. A rebirth was needed, a renewal of the quest.

The Renaissance proved to be just that: a rebirth of civilization. It presaged a renewal in commerce and culture, in philosophy and in science. The Crusades gave a rough beginning, but they also sparked the European imagination with exposure to the Muslim Middle East and an exotic Asia beyond. Islamic scholars had preserved the essence of Classical philosophy and already founded the first universities; these likewise spread interest into Europe. Beginning in Italy, city-states became wealthy and then nation-states grew strong. But with the strengthening of society there was no matching strengthening of the individual to balance it. Renaissance art may have glorified the individual, but this was only for the wealthy few who could afford to be patrons. Still the serfs were tied to the land, still the many were dominated by the few, still society was lord over the self.(19)

The ideas and inventions of the Renaissance in the 1600's led eventually to the Industrial Revolution in the 1800's. Wealth accumulated into power centers, society continued the shift from spiritual to material concerns, and people increasingly looked at their environment objectively rather than subjectively. Rather than being a part of their world, they became apart from it. Increasing wealth funded increasing discoveries and inventions, leading in turn to increasing focus on the material. This was matched with decreasing attention to the individual and decreasing attention to the self. As depicted in the old cinema classic, "Metropolis" and in Charlie Chaplin's "Modern Times," the individual became merely a cog in the machine, a small piece in the apparatus of society with no personal identity.

Our modern society maintains this spiritual loss of self even with tremendous improvements to our physical lives. We have more, yet we cannot be more. We live longer lives, but they are not greater lives. We have physical well-being with medical advances and nutritional improvements but little spiritual well-being. We have cures but not health, healing but not wholeness.

The rule of the corporate entity over the individual has become our modern version of the lord over the serf mentality. In Medieval society, most people sacrificed their own fulfillment and their own personal being for the gain of a few elite individuals. In modern society, most people sacrifice their own fulfillment and their personal being for the gain of a few multi-national corporations. The king has become the corporation, and the political rule of monarchy has become the economic rule of oligarchy.

This is perhaps nowhere more evident than in the rise and fall of Ken Lay and Enron, an historical reality that serves as a myth for our society. Enron became a rich corporation not by actually producing anything but rather by manipulating their markets, the ultimate example of power by control. Ken Lay, as the corporate king of Enron, was internationally acclaimed, a featured speaker at political conventions and a welcome member of numerous boards and charitable agencies. But the market manipulation couldn't last forever. The Enron collapse took with it the lifetime savings of thousands of employees, who were first told there was no risk or scandal and then denied the opportunity to cash their stocks while the corporate executives were liquidating their own shares. With the collapse of the corporation came the collapse of its king, and in the midst of convictions and appeals, Ken Lay died of a heart attack. The land and the king, the corporation and its executive, are one. But it is the people who suffer.

As primitives, we were at one with the world around us and all we viewed we saw as sacred. As children we approached the world with awe and wonder, with a sense of joy rather than a drive to control. With the rise of civilization and the advance of human technology, our lives are more comfortable but less meaningful. As adults we have learned to control more of our environment, but this too comes with a cost. We learn too late that anything we seek to control, we cannot enjoy. These two are mutually exclusive. In desiring to control something, I must separate myself from it and regard it as an object. In desiring to enjoy something, I must see myself as living in relationship with it, participating with it in a way that might lead to joy. Even the desire to control, whether we attain it or not, eliminates the possibility to enjoy. Of course, seeking the joy likewise does not guarantee its attainment, but seeking control eliminates the possibility of joy. We can seek either the joy or the control. It is one or the other; we cannot have both.

Our Declaration of Independence announces the inalienable rights of life, liberty and the pursuit of happiness. In our own times, we may have abandoned the pursuit of happiness for the pursuit of pleasure, only to realize that passing pleasures do not lead to lasting happiness. Too often, we seek immediate personal physical gratification, even to the detriment of everything else.

Seeking immediate personal physical gratification can be like eating cotton candy instead of a well balanced meal: it pleases the taste buds, but leaves the body wanting more. Immediate pleasure is like a bubbling brook, and lasting joy is like the current of a mighty river. It may look less exciting, but beneath the surface there flows a great strength.

We long for a life with meaning and purpose, a life of substance. We live empty lives that outwardly shine and sparkle, but it is fool's gold, not true gold, and covers only a hollow shell. There is within us a hungering, a longing, a desire that we experience but cannot express, a thing that will not be named. To name it is to control it, and it will not be controlled. We are filled but not fulfilled, busy yet bored, possessing all things yet lacking. There is within us a seeking for something that we cannot name, a desiring for a taste we cannot describe, a longing for something we try to ignore but cannot deny. It is the dilemma of our existence: we seek to be and to become. It is the pilgrimage of our personhood.

The Call to Pilgrimage: A Quest for Self

To be human means, to some extent, to be born to wander. The first modern humans, Homo Sapiens, have their roots in ancient Africa. Beginning less than 100,000 years ago, less than a tick on the cosmic clock, we began migrating from our African Eden and managed to find our way to the Americas around 20,000 years ago. All this without the aid of modern transportation! It seems from the time we became erect, we've been walking.

Human history may be described as a perpetual pilgrimage, an eternal wandering: physically, mentally and spiritually. The wandering is not because we are lost; the pilgrim is one who wanders with a purpose. As J.R.R. Tolkein wrote, "Not all who wander are lost."(20)

This wandering was done without having a set destination determined in advance. Without knowing where we were going, we were walking and wandering. Not because we had a goal, but because something in our guts compelled us. We walked with no maps or compass and only the horizon to guide us, for it was the horizon that called us. It seemed we were pilgrims, with the Peregrine falcon: always on the way, never arriving, always traveling, never settling.

Primitive societies have continued the tradition pilgrimage. The American Indians have their "Vision

Quest," when the lone warrior sets off on a trek for a goal that is more spiritual than physical and as much inward as outward. The Australian Aborigines have their "walkabouts," with much the same focus. The journey is as much about finding the self as it is exploring the environment.

In the Middle Ages, it became common place to know someone who was on pilgrimage or had been. Medieval writers record villages seemingly emptied of residents who had all gone off in pilgrimage, and of roadways seemingly teeming with hoards of pilgrims. It was a time of great devotion as people made pilgrimage to holy sites. Being on pilgrimage was also a way to get off the land and away from the confines and drudgery of serfdom that was at least tolerated, if not fully acceptable. Pilgrimage offered escape from the role of servant, relief from monotony of never ending chores, satisfaction of curiosities and freedom from one's own parish system.

The call of the Crusades was, in part, to make pilgrimage. Armed and militant, yes, but pilgrimage nonetheless, for the destination was nothing other than the land they called "Holy." To travel from the land that is home to the land that is holy is the very definition of pilgrimage.

The long ocean treks of the Vikings were sea going pilgrimages, as much for adventure and discovery as for plunder. The later voyages, to the New World and circumnavigating the globe, similarly give evidence to the desire for renewal that can be societal as well as personal. Simply calling the Americas "The New World" states the desire for renewal. The physical wandering is an expression of a spiritual longing. To be human means to be born to wander.

Joseph Campbell, renowned author on the myths of the world, in his greatest work, <u>The Hero with a Thousand Faces</u>, writes of this subconscious pilgrimage as adventure and testings on a heroic scale.(21) The myths of Babylonia and Egypt, of Greece and Rome, of India and China and the Americas, all share the archetype of pilgrimage as a means of self-discovery.

In more recent times, Carl Jung and Viktor Frankl write on the modern search for personal meaning. Jung writes of the individual's quest for self-knowledge and posits that every encounter from mid-life on is a search for meaning.(22) Frankl argues that the will to find meaning in our life is part of the essence of what makes us human.(23)

Philosophically, this builds on the groundwork of the Existentialists. Existentialism seeks to find meaning in existence and values the individual and subjectivity over objectivity. As a result, questions regarding the meaning of life and subjective experience are seen as being of paramount importance.(24)

Freedom of our choices and responsibility for those choices form the dread and the desire of our existence. Believing that our existence has meaning and purpose, or persevering in spite of life's perceived meaninglessness, forms the basis upon which we maintain our sanity and seek our serenity.

From the beginning of our species, to be human means to be seeking, to be searching. We wandered from the plains of Africa until we blanketed the planet, traveling at such a pace that our forebearers must have been constantly trekking. We traveled as hunter-gatherers, eating on the run from the very beginning. Maybe drive-ins and carry-outs are simply a modern expression of our primeval wanderlust!

With the birth of agriculture came the rise of civilization and our first step toward a more sedentary lifestyle. Instead of hunter-gatherers we became farmer-settlers. But a few among us continued to venture, continued to hunt, continued to explore. They became heroes for us, and the stuff of myth and legend. These lone individuals, who carried on the quest, became outer expressions of our own inner yearnings, the longing that was part of our bones, the desires that was wired into our DNA. From the time we became settled and civilized, we began the tradition of pilgrimage, of an outward and visible manifestation of the inner and spiritual longing of our souls.

The desire for meaning and purpose in our lives, whether in terms of myth and religion or of psychology, is an expression of what it means to be "spiritual." To be spiritual means to believe, to hope or hunch, that there must be more to our life than that which surrounds us, there is more to our existence than the mere experience of it, that there is a meaning behind it, a purpose that guides it. We may call it karma or destiny or fate, the influence of the stars or the hands of the gods. We may call our spiritual guides Isis or Jesus, Moses or Mohammed, Buddha or Balder. Through it all, one truth speaks out: to be human is to be in process, on the way. To be human is to be a pilgrim, a traveler of the soul.

A pilgrimage is an outer journey with an inner goal: to know one's self. It is a journey that by its very definition means it will take a lifetime. A pilgrimage is to travel with the soul as well as the body. A pilgrimage is a journey without boundaries, for the journey is always within.

As the Peregrine is born for its flight, we are also born for our own journey. We also are born with a questing spirit and an inquisitive mind, born with imagination to dream and a will to act, courage to dare. The call to pilgrimage has been heard and heeded throughout recorded history. It is a call that we ignore at our own peril.

Pilgrimages of the Ancients

The myths of primitive religions and the legends of ancient civilizations are filled with stories of travelers who venture forth, who make their lives an adventure and their existence a quest. In the works of Carl Jung and Joseph Campbell, these are pilgrims who are heroes and heroes who are pilgrims.(25)

The wandering that populated our planet was a form of pilgrimage, an exploration in space and time that led to a discovery of self. From the time we became erect, we have been wandering, and this wandering has been a journey of the spirit as well as the flesh. As our outer lives became more settled, our inner wanderings continued. This wanderlust of the soul was expressed through myths and legends, expression of the imagination and rituals that became part of the fabric of our religions. The concept of Pilgrimage has always had a religious or spiritual undercurrent.

Our spirituality is a part of who we are. It is as natural, normal and innate as is our emotion or intellect. Our spiritual longing is as much a part of what makes us human as is our inquisitive curiosity. Our spirituality is also quite personal; it is part of what makes us persons. Spirituality takes many forms and expressions. Religion is the institutionalization of our spirituality; religion gives spirituality structure. It may be said that religion is the skeleton that holds spirituality together; spirituality is the muscle that gives religion energy. The two are in symbiotic relationship. Without the structure provided by religious organization and institution, spirituality devolves into an amorphous blob. Without the muscle and vitality of spirituality, religious structures become nothing but dead bones. It takes both bones and muscle for a body to walk; it takes both religion and spirituality for a person to become a pilgrim in their life.

Pilgrimage is a physical journey with a spiritual purpose, it has an inner goal and destination just as it has an outer one. The pilgrimages of the ancients were journeys toward a destination. Upon reaching that destination, the pilgrimage was ended and the pilgrim returned home. But the expectation was that arriving at the destination would also achieve a greater, more noble purpose. Reaching the destination would initiate a change in the person, a change not physical as the change in place, but a spiritual change, a change in soul. The person who returned from the pilgrimage would not be the same as the person who began the journey, just as Joseph Campbell's hero was changed by successfully accomplishing his or her adventure.(26) This is what Turner describes as ritual and Eliade describes as sacred.(27) Sacred time and ritual space is that time and space that transforms and defines us; it is where we find ourselves, lose ourselves and become ourselves. It is transcendent time and space. Sacred time and ritual space is where we encounter the height and depth and breadth of life in all its fullness. It is where the primitive would see through the eyes of the Peregrine and fly with its wings. The person, being changed, would see their home from a new and fresh perspective; because they were changed, for them all had changed.

The ancient Greeks would make pilgrimages to the Oracle at Delphi, making a physical journey with a spiritual purpose. They came seeking divine wisdom, a spiritual discernment that would give them direction for their lives. The Oracle spoke the words of the gods and expressed the will of the gods. Upon return, the pilgrims had not just seen the sights and heard the sounds, they had gained divine wisdom and knew the will of the gods for their lives.

The adventures of Perseus and Hercules are physical adventures, but described with divine purpose, undertaken at the behest of the Gods, given to the heroes that they may prove themselves, to the Gods and to themselves. The stories of these adventures were a way for their hearers to understand all life as a holy journey, a divine undertaking, a spiritual adventure.

Upon the legalization of their faith by Constantine the Great, Christians began making pilgrimages. Constantine's mother, Helen, traveled to Jerusalem to walk the steps that Jesus walked in the places where he walked them, to travel the Via Dolorosa, to see the Place of the Skull described in sacred text carved into the hills of Golgotha, to find the remnants of the True Cross. She began the trips to the Holy Land that have become a bulwark for the travel industry and a boon for the nation of Israel.

Etheria was a Spanish nun in the 5th century who kept a diary of her travels during her own pilgrimage to Jerusalem.(28) She writes of the sights and sounds, places and people along the way, as one would expect in a travelogue. She also liberally mixes in quotes and paraphrases of Scripture liberally and draws spiritual insight from her physical journey. Half of her journal is her travels, half of it recounts the liturgies of the worship services she attends in and around Jerusalem. All of it draws spiritual recollections from the experience. One can hear the echoes of Etheria in John Climacus, John of Mt. Sinai, in his writing a century later, Ladder of Divine Ascent.(29)

Of her ascent of Mt. Sinai, she says, "The toil was great, for I had to go up on foot, the ascent being impossible in the saddle. And yet I did not feel the toil on the side of the ascent, because I realized that the desire which I had was being fulfilled by God." (30)

The physical exertion is eased by the spiritual benefit, the toil of the flesh is driven by the desire of the soul. In the process of her physical ascent, she was also drawing closer to God. Through her physical travel, and even travail, her spiritual desire was being fulfilled. This is the essence of pilgrimage.

Our modern, western, view of pilgrimage is based upon and developed from this and other similar experiences. Pilgrimage includes both a physical and a spiritual exploration, a physical journey driven by spiritual desires and for spiritual benefit. Yet it is a physical journey, with beginning and ending, with destination and goal. The outset of the journey is clearly marked and its conclusion plainly noted. It is an adventure that is accomplished.

The journey has an impact upon the traveler, the pilgrim becomes a changed person upon their return. But the journey has definite boundaries. When Etheria set out, she set her eyes toward Jerusalem. When Jason began his adventures, he knew he pursued the golden fleece. Without arriving at Jerusalem, Etheria's pilgrimage would not have been completed. Without attaining his prize, Jason's adventure would not have been successful.

The physical journey is not all there is, but it is nonetheless real, and its successful completion is a necessary part of fulfilling the pilgrimage. The inner journey is a necessary part of the pilgrimage, and that element that distinguishes the pilgrimage from general travel, but the inner journey alone is not enough. The spiritual pilgrimage cannot be fulfilled without also completing the outer journey. This is our commonly accepted pattern for pilgrimage in the West.

Pilgrimage East and West

Pilgrimage has been a constant and universal element of human civilization, in all times and places. We were born wanderers and in our hearts we still long to wander. As soon as our hunter-gatherer ancestors became farmer-settlers, we have looked to the horizon beyond and surveyed the landscape within. The earliest civilizations of Egypt, Mesopotamia, India and China recorded tales of heroes who went off on adventures to discover themselves. These civilizations likewise found rituals and symbols to claim the sacredness of life and the holiness of daily existence.

Muslims are expected to make their Hajj at least once during their life. This journey is such an important commitment that it is one of the foundational principles of their faith. The Hajj is a pilgrimage to Mecca during the holy month of Ramadan, a period of fasting during the day and feasting during the night.(31) In Mecca, the pilgrims participate in numerous rituals and re-enactments to build them up in their faith. It was during a Hajj that Malcom X was motivated to leave the Nation of Islam of Elijah Muhammed and Black Muslims of the United States to adopt a more universal form of Islam compatible with the global Islamic community.(32) Clearly, the Hajj as pilgrimage has power to renew and transform lives.

The Hindus are noted for their annual pilgrimages to the Ganges and other rivers, all regarded as holy. The Ganges is considered a flowing ladder to heaven; bathing in it is purifying and restorative. Pilgrimage is a time when the devotee turns their life over to celebrate and enact the lives of the gods; they are journeys into sacred time and place. Rather than a trip to one particular holy site, as is the case of Jerusalem in Christianity and Mecca in Islam, the Hindu pilgrimage visits a number of holy sites, each with their rituals to be reenacted.(33) Different as it may be, the act of pilgrimage is nonetheless an important part of the Hindu faith; the movement itself is a sacred act. One of their texts reads, "Flower-like the heels of the wanderer, the body growing and fruitful; all sins disappear, slain by the toil of wandering."(34) For the Hindu, the act of pilgrimage is intended to mediate between the disciplines of awareness in this present world and detachment from it. This balance prepares them for their perpetual pilgrimage from life to life through reincarnation.

Buddhist pilgrimage is a reenactment of the life of Buddha, whether in actual physical geography or in the imagination. According to sacred text, Buddha himself prescribed pilgrimages to the place of his birth, of his enlightenment, where he preached his first sermon and where he died, attaining Nirvana.(35) By extension, other events in his life and in the history of Buddhism have been added as appropriate sites for pilgrimage. Pilgrimage is a metaphor for the path to enlightenment; it is a means of renouncing one's own world and history and opening up to the reality of the spiritual world. If one dies while on pilgrimage, one is specially blessed and assured of Nirvana. In Japan, ascending Mt. Fuji is a form of pilgrimage that is both patriotic and religious.(36) In Buddhism, pilgrimage is a way both to honor the past and

the faith of our ancestors and also to follow one's own path to enlightenment, physically and spiritually.

All the world religions have incorporated the discipline of pilgrimage into their practices, just as every human civilization has found a way to express our innate longing to wander and incorporate this wanderlust through social institutions.

Pilgrimage in medieval Europe was also an important expression of personal devotion, but the social structure of fiefdom and serfdom was not conducive to the extended pilgrimages to Jerusalem or even Rome. Alternatives needed to be found. A great labyrinth was built into the floor of the nave of Chartres Cathedral in the 13th century. Walking to Chartres and this labyrinth was considered equivalent to a pilgrimage.(37) The path of the labyrinth, traveled in devotion, gave the mind opportunity to focus on the needs of the spirit instead of the body. It offers a physical manifestation of the spiritual path. A labyrinth is a specific type of maze in which there is only one way in, which leads to the center, and then back. It is not a maze wherein one gets lost, but rather where one gets found. The labyrinth at Chartres is composed of eleven concentric circles, but a large number of labyrinths were constructed in a variety of configurations. A seven circuit labyrinth was also quite popular. Labyrinths can be found throughout Europe. The Neolithic graves at Newgrange, dating from 3500 B.C., are decorated with three conjoined circles, each of which is composed of layers of concentric circles.(38) Labyrinths can be found in use today as a way to make walking devotions and to experience the sense of pilgrimage.

Even our secular society has found ways to incorporate pilgrimage. Fans of Elvis Presley have made

trips to his home at Graceland an important part of the tourist trade for Memphis that has significant impact on the local economy. The Parrot-head fans of Jimmy Buffet make the tours of his band to become a modern form of pilgrimage, where they enter into a different existence, a different understanding of time and space, a different expression of their lives. The Deadheads, fans of the Grateful Dead, created the same ritualistic observance of that band's tours long after the band ceased to be listed on the popular charts. They would set up entire communities of followers in the fields surrounding the band's performance. Groupies have been a part of Rock and Roll almost as long as the musical form has existed. Sports fans make pilgrimage to the fields of play of their champions. Amateur historians visit the battlefields of the Civil War or the American Revolution. Hikers make a life goal of walking the Appalachian Trail. Whether we consider ourselves religious or not, the call to pilgrimage is a part of who we are as human beings. It is part of our psyche, part of our soul, part of our spirit.

There is so much evidence from so many different sources and throughout human history demonstrating that we are an animal meant to wander, a creature called to seek, that it simply cannot be denied. The question is not "Are we on pilgrimage?" but rather "How can we satisfy our need to be in pilgrimage?"

From beyond the beginning of time, in any conceptual sense, we have been wandering. From the time we first became erect, we have been wandering. Throughout our primeval history and all around the globe, we have been wandering. In all our ancient civilizations, we have had pilgrims: people taking outer, physical journeys with an inner, spiritual purpose. Every religion has included

pilgrimage as a part of its practice: ancient and modern, Eastern and Western. Contemporary society has found a multiplicity of expressions of the call to pilgrimage, making the most secular activities to be expressions of this spiritual quest.

Given that we are spiritual beings, seeking meaning and purpose in our lives, wanting to wander, to be somehow "on the way", with a sense of determination and destiny, how can we best go about it? Given that we are pilgrims, how can we be on pilgrimage, in our own time and place? Is there a form of pilgrimage that can inform our practice and transform our existence? Can we yet learn from the Peregrine?

Celtic Pilgrimage: Wandering from Birth to Rising

All the patterns of pilgrimage that we have examined thus far have been substantially the same: there is a beginning point, an ending point and the journey itself. In all pilgrimages, the journey is to be inward as well as outward. But the journey ends once the destination is attained. Following this, there is only the return. The aim of all pilgrimage is not just to make the journey but also for personal transformation, so that the person that is returning is different from the one that left. This is the pattern for Greek and Roman, for Indian and Chinese.

The ancient Celts had a different pattern. The Celtic pattern for pilgrimage focused less on the destination and more on the journey. In fact, for the Celts, the focus of the pilgrimage was never to arrive at the destination, but rather to be "on the way."

The Celts did not live in cities; they lived in villages, farming settlements, places where hunter-gatherers and farmer-settlers could meet. The Celts did not worship in cathedrals or great temples; they worshiped in groves of sacred oaks and in stone circles made holy by blessing and use. Their nave was nature itself, their canopy all creation. Their sacred space was all beneath the sky; their holy time declared in each passing breath.(39)

Much of the Celtic world was over-run by the Roman, first by the legions of the Roman Empire and later by the legions of clergy in the Roman Catholic Church. But the Celts held on to the fringe of Europe, the hinterland Rome did not want or could not control: Ireland, Scotland, Wales, Cornwall, the Isle of Man, Brittany in France and Gallicia in Spain. The Celts converted to Christianity, but it was a conversion done peacefully, without the sword or martyrdom and without abandoning their Celtic roots.(40)

Visiting Ireland today, one is struck by the abundance of holy sites. It seems every hill was blessed by Patrick and every well by Brigit. Fields are scattered about with standing stones or with dolmen, ancient burial sites where leprechauns were once thought to hide and treasures could be found. Every place is just "a wee walk" away. A pilgrim could spend a lifetime wandering the island from sacred site to sacred site and still not see it all, which was precisely the goal of Celtic pilgrimage: always to be on pilgrimage. A pilgrim is one who is on pilgrimage, not one who has arrived.

Ireland was converted without loss of blood, but the Irish did devise a scheme of martyrdom. Black martyrdom was that of death and red martyrdom that of shedding blood or suffering for one's faith, both of which had been denied them. But green martyrdom was that of hermitage.

n Irish monk would go off to be alone, as did the monks of the East, the desert fathers and mothers, that so greatly influenced the Irish. But Ireland is not a desert and the Irish could not be true hermits. Instead of the dry desolation of the desert, Ireland is green and moist, verdant and fertile. One goes off to be alone, and then another monk says, "I'll go off and be alone with him."

Then another and another and another. Pretty soon, you have a whole community of monks "being alone together." The monks of Skellig Michael modeled themselves after those of Mt. Athos with some success, maintaining a secluded community for 600 years, but for most, seclusion from others was simply not possible.(41) Green martyrdom was always short-lived.

White martyrdom was the worst kind for the Irish, the most difficult and sacrificial. White martyrdom was that of abandoning one's hearth and home and committing the rest of earthly existence to wandering as a pilgrim, always traveling, never arriving, and never returning home again. White martyrdom was that of self-exile, and abandoning one's life always to being on pilgrimage.(42)

The Celtic Christians were greatly influenced by the Eastern church and felt a particular affinity with it.(43) The monastic communities in Ireland were laid out following the pattern of the desert communities in Syria, Palestine and Egypt, even to the point of similar architectural styles. The Eastern dating of Easter was followed, rather than the Roman; an issue that became a major point of contention as Rome exerted its authority over the Celtic Christians. They did not see themselves as establishing an independent Celtic Christian tradition, although some of that did happen. In the period from 400 A.D. to 1200 A.D., the time of the Celtic Christian experience, travel was hazardous and communication difficult. Independence could be accidentally established. In spite of the risks, travel between the East and Ireland is in very strong evidence. Pilgrimage became a pattern for life.

The story is told of a band of monks setting off on pilgrimage in a coracle, a shallow nearly round sailboat.

They set off without oar or rudder, only letting the wind blow them where it will. Upon landing in England, they set off on foot across the land. Soon they were overtaken by the local lord's guards, who arrested them and brought them before him as spies. In his interrogation, he demanded where they were from and where they were bound. The first they freely shared. The second, they could not know. They had no destination; they were simply "on pilgrimage." The point of pilgrimage is to be on the way, not to have arrived.(45)

Patrick, the patron saint of Ireland, was born in England, carried into slavery in Ireland as a boy, and later returned willingly as a man, to bring the Irish he knew to the Christ he served. He spent his life in Ireland traveling to all the petty kings and the great kings, bringing to them his Good News.(46) In his "Letter to Coroticus," written late in life, he describes himself as "a stranger and an exile,"(47) always on the way, but never arriving.

Columba was born a prince, raised a druid and became a priest, believing that those three were not mutually exclusive.(48) He fought a battle to win a psalter, costing the lives of 3,000 warriors. In remorse, he exiled himself from his beloved home and took refuge on the isle of Iona, off the large island of Mull, off the western coast of Scotland. He built an abbey there, formed a community and became a bishop and saint. It was from Iona that the Celtic monks traveled throughout Europe, re-Christianizing it after the fall of Rome and the barbarian invasions, described in Thomas Cahill's aptly named book, How the Irish saved Civilization.(49) Columba spent his life as a pilgrim, never again seeing his home.

Columbanus was one of the greatest of Columba's disciples, spending his life traveling throughout what is now modern Germany, Belgium, France, Austria and northern Italy. He founded monasteries and established communities. One of these was Bobbio, in northern Italy, a place that figures predominantly in the conversion and education of St. Francis.(50) There is a spiritual connection between the followers of Francis and the Celtic Christians, in their joy of living and in their unity with nature.

Brendan the Navigator was another Irish monk and pilgrim and adventurer. He spent years plying the north Atlantic in his tiny coracles, engaged in physical exploration and spiritual discovery. In the record of his travels, he describes Iceland, Greenland and North America. He describes visiting Hell and singing with angels. Clearly, this is a physical journey with spiritual significance.(51)

During the early Middle Ages, the Celts of Ireland earned a reputation for their pilgrimage. Stories were told of villages being emptied of their residents in Ireland and the countryside of France and of Italy covered with them. The time finally came, in the 14th century, when the Irish were forbidden to leave their island.(52) Seven trips to Glendalough, the holy site for St. Kevin, was equivalent with a pilgrimage to Rome.(53) Climbing Croagh Patrick was compared to a sharing in Christ's temptations.(54) The Irish suffered these restrictions and substitutions well. For them, the point had never been about the destination anyway. Like the flight of the Peregrine Falcon, the pilgrimage is the journey, not the destination.

The orders of Mendicants in the late Middle Ages may well have been inspired by the example of Celtic pilgrims. The Mendicants emphasized both service and poverty and balanced contemplation with action. Following the example of the Irish, the wandering Mendicants claimed no home but the highway and no calling but to travel. They lived by begging what they could from the charity of others. This, too was a problem in the Middle Ages. A society fixed by place and role could little afford pilgrims wandering about, owning no place and owing no role.(55)

The ancient Celts had spread from the heart of Europe to its extremities. The Christian Celts carried their wanderlust with them into their new-found faith. The Celtic monks traveled Europe, reseeding it with their faith. The Irish became famous as a pilgrim people, always traveling to holy sites and in a way that made the traveling itself holy. They dedicated their lives to being "on the way." Celtic pilgrimage is not like that of other cultures, where there is always a destination and an ending to the pilgrimage. For the Celts, life was a pilgrimage from the place of their birthing to the place of their rising. Inspired by the Celts, life for us may be a pilgrimage, from the place of our birthing to the place of our rising!

A Pilgrim People

We are a people born to wander, born to be pilgrims. The pilgrimage of the Peregrine is from winter to summer, from nesting to hunting. Our pilgrimage as humans is our search for meaning and purpose in our lives.

Every four year old is a natural philosopher, asking "Why?" Why do we do this, why do we go there, why do we do what we do the way we do? The basic question of philosophy is "Why?" There is no other word that comes more instinctually off our tongues. In this sense, we are all Existentialists.

From Kierkegaard through Sartre, Existentialists have pushed us on the "Why" question. "Why are we here? What is the meaning and purpose of our existence? Is there one? How do we know? How can we tell?" Kierkegaard's answer was the leap of faith, to believe in spite of our unbelief and lack of proof. Sartre concluded there was no reason, no purpose, yet we live regardless.(56)

What reason do most people seem to find to justify their existence? Why do most people seem to be here? What is the motivation for their existence? What gets them out of bed in the morning?

Judging by the lifestyles we see, most people in the West seem to be here to consume and acquire, or to be entertained. We're up early in the morning, slug down a cup of coffee and shove a bagel down our throat, then out the door, in the car, onto the expressway for the morning commute. We begin the day by waiting in line. We wait in line in our cars, lined up all the way from the suburbs to the city. We'll eat and drink, talk on our phones, work on our computers, all while also driving the car. We do half a dozen things simultaneously, but are never really present to any one of them. Work itself becomes a pastime, a drudgery. We work to earn our credit, so we can consume and acquire.

Shopping malls are the true temples of our society. We've laughed at the saying, "When the going gets tough, the tough go shopping." Yet after September 11th, President Bush urged all patriotic Americans to support their country by doing just that, go shopping.

What do we value? What do we spend our time, our money and our energy on? Is it on stuff or on substance, on material or on meaning, on pleasure or on purpose? If we take those questions seriously and apply them to our own lives, we may be forced to acknowledge how superficial and transient we have become.

We work hard all day long at jobs that drain us rather than fulfill us, that empty us instead of energizing us. At the end of the day, we collapse exhausted like lumps of flesh in front of our televisions, barely mustering enough energy to work the remote.

We build larger and larger homes, buy sport utility vehicles that won't fit in our oversized garages, and rent storage cubicles to hold all the extra stuff we have that is too dear to us to part with, so that we can go out and buy more stuff. We exist to consume, acquire and be entertained.

Our lives are busy and bored, hectic and empty. Our calendars are filled; our lives our empty. We have beautiful houses, but they are not homes. We have a mother, a father and 2.3 children, but they are not a family, with relationships and interconnected lives.

A generation ago, children were sometimes disciplined by being sent to their room, a form of solitary confinement within the family. Today's children have all they need in their rooms: telephone, television, computer, mini-refrigerator, etc. Being sent to their room is equivalent to being sent to their own private Disneyworld.

Our nation expresses our culture's quest for power, for control, yet there is little lasting joy, only passing pleasures. We have forgotten that we cannot enjoy anything that we seek to control. Even the desire for control, whether it is attained or not, eliminates the possibility for joy. If we would have joy, we must first abandon even the desire to control.

Our culture lies starved before our eyes and we do not see. Margaret Mead, famous anthropologist, purportedly described the United States as a "ritually starved society."(57) She spent years studying societies of Polynesia, societies that maintained rituals that filled their lives with meaning. Unlike the primitives around the world today or those of our own past, we have stripped our rituals of meaning, denied rituals that have fed us through the generations, and then created artificial rituals, rituals empty of meaning. We create rituals for the beginning of junior high basketball games and avoid rituals that speak to our heart and soul.

Robert Moore adds the insights of Victor Turner, Mircea Eliade and Joseph Campbell to his own experience as psycho-therapist, arguing in support of Margaret Mead's claim. As a culture, we have deprived ourselves of the sacred space and the ritual process that we need for our own personal transformation. We suffer individually and as a society by this lack. Indeed, our vitality as a civilization depends upon our ability to revision spiritual leadership in a way that is appropriate for the 21st century.(58)

There is more than the physical to being human and more than our immediate surroundings to our world. We know we have emotions and thoughts. These are real to us even though they have no physical existence. Our thoughts lead to action that can determine the course of our lives. Our emotions have the ability to inspire or to destroy us. We ignore them at our peril.

We've all stood at the refrigerator, door ajar, scanning its teeming contents, finding nothing that fills us. Maybe it's not the stomach that is hungry. We live in a country that is monstrously overweight and all indications are that the increase itself will increase. It's not the stomach that is empty; it's the soul.

Conversely, we have exercise clubs appearing on every street. We work out, pump iron, stretch and sweat with our bodies. What can't be worked out, we cut out. Cosmetic surgeons are kept busy fixing perceived flaws with our outer, physical appearance. What of the soul, the spirit, the heart, the inner being?

Whether we are fat or fit, both focus on the physical. Is there more to us than the flesh? Our greatest minds throughout the history of Western civilization have believed so. Socrates, the originator of philosophy as a discipline, believed the search for meaning was nothing less than a quest for the divine and that the unexamined life was not worth living.(59) Isaac Newton, the father of modern science, wrote more on religion and the Bible than all of his scientific dissertations combined.(60) Albert Einstein, perhaps the greatest mind of the last century, said, "I want to know God's thoughts, the rest are mere details." Part of what makes us human is the search for the sacred, the hunger for the holy.(61)

Carl Jung, one of the original pioneers of psychotherapy, believed that the spiritual quest or the religious instinct was an essential part of our humanity and that its roots lie buried deep within our subconscious, undiscovered self.(62) Our salvation hinges upon our integrity, our explorations of that undiscovered country within and literally incorporating it, giving it flesh and blood, making it part of our body, so that we may become an integrated whole. Our pilgrimage, then, is within. Not on the crowded expressways, not in the crowded city centers, but the inner way, the journey to the center of our soul.

Viktor Frankl, physician, psychotherapist and survivor of the Nazi concentration camps, developed his theory of Logotherapy as the third Viennese school of Psychotherapy.(63) As the Existentialists argue, we are faced with life's transitoriness. The past is over, the future is not yet here. All that is real is the present, and it is fleeting. We are faced with temporality and mortality. Logotherapy contends that this transitoriness of life gives us possibilities for meaningful fulfillment, opportunities to create and experience, even to suffer meaningfully. Our life may last only 70 or 80 years, our thoughts and dreams may last mere seconds, but each one, having been, exists for eternity. Once the thought, the act, the dream has been called into being, it continues to exist on its own for all eternity. Life becomes a life-long question and answer period, for which we can respond only by and through our lives. Responding to life, to the bare fact of our existence, means being responsible for our lives.

Life is a pilgrimage, from the place of our birthing to the place of our rising. We are born to be pilgrims, Peregrines. Our purpose, our meaning, is not in our destination but in our journey. To be human is to be a pilgrim; to be a pilgrim is to be on pilgrimage. Our pilgrimage is nothing less than our quest for meaning in our lives.

The fault with all the other models of pilgrimage and the reason they fail us today is because they all focus on attaining a goal, on arriving at a destination. Greek and Roman, Hindu and Buddhist, the Muslim Hajj, the Roman Catholic images of pilgrimage all focus on arriving at a site, journeying to an outward, physical goal, a goal that is attainable and achievable. It is a journey that transforms the pilgrim, it is an outward physical journey with an inner spiritual purpose, but it is still one that ends.

If life is a pilgrimage, then its only true ending is in the dying. Our goal becomes our grave. If we are to convert our existentialist dilemma into a pilgrimage of purpose, then our goal is our grave, our destination is our death. This is an end that comes only at the end, certainly the end of time as we know it. The journey toward a physical location that is a part of these other pilgrimages is not the point. The journey that is inward, that centers on our soul, becomes the one pilgrimage that can consume and contain our life, that can direct and guide it. By definition, it takes a lifetime to discover the meaning of a lifetime: it must be lived before it can be learned.

The Celtic model for pilgrimage becomes the one model that can fulfill our lives, that can feed our spiritual hunger, that can become a model, a paradigm, an archetype, for our inner journey in the search for meaning in our existence. Celtic pilgrimage is about the journey, not the destination. It proclaims that we are pilgrims, and as pilgrims we are by definition on pilgrimage. Our pilgrimage is the journey of our lives, each day being one step along the way. We journey from our birthing to our rising. Like the Peregrine falcon, we are born to fly, to soar, to wander, to travel, to seek the horizon.

To Grow in One Place

Some may read this dissertation on pilgrimage as a pattern for life and wonder about the purpose of the monastic vows of chastity, poverty and especially stability. If we are made for the pilgrimage, the quest for meaning, then what is the function of vows to stay in one place? How does the call to stability relate to the yearning to wander?

The vow of stability is a long respected element of the monastic tradition. For the monastic community, staying in one place is a vital ingredient for personal spiritual growth, rather than always being on the move. A saying that describes this is, "A transplanted tree does not have deep roots."(64)

These need not be opposing views; they can be complementary. Certainly, there is room for both traditions to exist in our world. Both stress the importance of living fully in the present moment, of being aware of and engaged by one's environment. Both view life as an experience of lived prayer, living into the divine presence that surrounds, sustains and penetrates us. Both seek understanding through self-knowledge. Both strive for balance in life and welcome toward others. Personal spiritual growth is available on either path; fulfillment is possible from either choice.

Monasticism grew out of the experiences of the desert fathers and mothers of the early church. With the establishment of Christianity as the official religion of the

Roman Empire by Constantine the Great in the Edicts of Toleration of 311 (65), many Christians shared a concern that the Church had become too worldly. They withdrew themselves into the desert, to fast and pray and wrestle with their temptations as Christ did in the beginning of his ministry. One of these prayer warriors was Arsenius, whose life became a model followed by thousands.

Arsenius was an educated Roman nobleman, who had been a tutor to the emperor's children and lived in the palace. In his personal devotions, he considered the way of salvation and heard a voice say, "Flee, be silent, pray always." These three actions became the focus for the rest of his life. He left the court, sailed to Alexandria and began a solitary life living in the desert. He learned the strength of silence and the power of prayer. His life was one that called others to withdraw from the world, enter their own inner silence, and live each incident of their lives as a call to prayer.(66)

The examples of the desert fathers and mothers served as a foundation for the development of monastic communities. The first monastic communities formed in the deserts of Syria, Palestine and Egypt where the first Christian hermits lived, and they offered a means to balance community and solitude. These communities gained strong reputations and wide interests and enjoyed influence far beyond their numbers or borders.

John Cassian was an early missionary for monasticism. Born in 360 A.D., in what is now Romania, he joined a monastery in Bethlehem then traveled to other monasteries before taking his monastic message and ideals into the western Roman Empire. In his Institutes and Conferences he writes at length on the individual and community disciplines of monasticism and the spiritual life. Cassian asserted that the monastic community was the ideal setting to form the foundation for personal spiritual growth. He also believed that once these disciplines had been established, the mature monk could become a spiritual pilgrim, traveling and living beyond the bounds of one's community. He believed that, while the vow of stability was a necessary part of spiritual formation, it need not be made for life; the solitude necessary for contemplation was something carried within one's self.(67)

Others who followed after Cassian were less confident in the spiritual growth of the solitary pilgrim or hermit; they formed communities with lifetime vows of stability. One of these was St. Benedict, who founded his monastery of Monte Cassino in 529 and is regarded as the Father of Western Monasticism. He composed a Rule for his monks and his monastery that is followed to this day by Benedictine Orders. In it, he details the life, relationships and discipline of the individuals and of the community.(68)

One of these disciplines is that of stability, the promise of the monk to remain in the community that accepted him until his death. Roving monks were seen as undisciplined and a threat to community life. The vow of stability brought mobility under the influence of obedience, and with it the hope of constancy and contentment.(69)

Monastic life with its vows of stability, chastity and poverty, all under the discipline of the abbot, has proven to be an appropriate and rewarding path toward experiencing the fullness of life in all moments. Perhaps the greatest example of this is Brother Lawrence of the Resurrection, as seen in his Practice of the Presence of

God. Brother Lawrence started as a mercenary, who was wounded and captured in battle. When he gained his freedom, he sought out a monastic community to join. The one he sought questioned the sincerity of his intentions, so brought him in but only as a lay brother, to tend the garden and work in the kitchen. Brother Lawrence took to his assigned tasks obediently and diligently, and used them as opportunities to pursue the fullness of God, occasions to experience the sanctity of life. The community noticed his devotion and late in his life asked him to write down his discipline. One line that is most descriptive is this: "I would not so much as stoop to pick up a straw from the ground but for the grace of God."(70)

Cassian commended the value of his own spiritual journey: joining a community, learning its discipline, and moving on when ready. Benedict commended the value of his spiritual journey: joining a community and dedicating one's life to growing within the framework of the discipline of the community. Brother Lawrence lived a life in the world before joining a community and dedicating the rest of his days to finding the divine presence in his everyday activities. Clearly, monasticism has been a way to find the sacredness in life, the holy in each moment. Just as clearly, there are a variety of expressions within monasticism that may be equally suited for different individuals. What is important is not the means used but the goal attained. As a way to discover the divine depths in our daily lives, how does the Celtic approach to pilgrimage compare?

To begin with, pilgrimage per se is not simply travelling or wandering around aimlessly. Any pilgrimage is by definition a journey with a mission, an outward journey with an inner and spiritual meaning. A pilgrimage is a journey with clear intention, with focused attention, with a sense of spiritual direction as well as geographic.

Most pilgrimages focus on a destination, their goal is to arrive. Celtic pilgrimage differs in that it is focused not on the destination but on the journey itself, on being aware of one's place in the present. To be (fully) present to the presence of the Present (of the divine) in the present. Celtic pilgrimage is not about the destination but rather living fully in the now. As Jesus said, "Let the day's own trouble be sufficient for the day."(Matthew 6:34) This intent, focused attention is no less a discipline than that of the traditional monastic disciplines, and one that monastics would support and emulate. The challenge to live deeply and openly in the moment is one that speaks to the faithful of all religions.

Celtic pilgrimage invites us to participate fully in the experience of life, to seek depth of meaning and clarity of vision in these experiences with openness and authenticity, and to welcome others freely along the way. We are all pilgrims, each of us finding and following our own path, but we are pilgrims together, and as such, can share the journey in community with others, growing in wisdom through this sharing.

Not all of us can accept the traditional vows of the monastery: chastity, poverty and stability. Not all of us want to accept them. The world we live in is fast paced and increasingly secular. The approach of Celtic pilgrimage as a path for life is one that can be adopted in the modern world and may serve to complement the world of the monastery. Celtic pilgrimage will never replace the monastery, nor is it intended to, but it does provide an alternate route toward the same goal: to be at one with the One, to comprehend the breadth and length and height and depth of life, to know what surpasses knowledge, and be filled with all the fullness of God. (Ephesians 3:18-19)

From the Earth to the Stars

Most of us live lives looking into the gutter. We are so caught up in the urgency of the immediacy that is right before our eyes that we are blind to anything beyond it, like children who hide the moon behind their thumb. The thumb may seem larger, more important, than the moon, but only because we lack perspective. We are as infants, thinking the world disappears when we close our eyes.

We are imprisoned in the now, controlled by the calendar, the clock, the schedule, the ipod and palm pilot. We live life by appointment, driven by agenda, controlled by meetings.

We are as serfs, born into the village, tilling the field, tied to the soil, plodding through the days of our lives. We are some one else's pet mice, running on treadmills. If the only way to win a rat race is to become a rat, what's the point? We get to the top of the ladder only to find its against the wrong building, the top of the heap but its still just a heap.

We are caterpillars crawling in the dirt, chewing on the leaves, never dreaming that we are born to become butterflies, flying high above it all. The stuff of our composition says that we are more. We are made of the stuff of the stars, and the call of the cosmos beckons us from within our own genes.

Inside us, we carry heavy metals. They are necessary for our own existence. Heavy metals are created in the heart and the heat of the stars. But heavy metals are not made in first generation stars. In order for there to be heavy metals, there must first be at least two generations of stars, each generation lasting billions of years. The first generation of stars creates some of the lighter elements. Only stars that are themselves composed of the stuff of previous stars are capable of producing heavy metals. These heavy metals are necessary in order for there to be human life on planet earth. We are made of the stuff of the stars!(71)

Some 15 to 18 billion years ago, the entire universe was incredibly small, a mere dot, and infinitely hot and dense. At some point and for some reason, it exploded in the "big bang." Space, time, energy and matter were created in an instant. First, the force of gravity was created, then the elements of matter. Not matter as we think of it, rather quarks, leptons, muons, neutrinos and photons, the stuff of quantum science.(72)

After 300,000 years, electrons gathered around nascent nuclei to form the first atoms. After another 700,000 years, all free electrons had been absorbed and the universe becomes transparent. After a billion years, the force of gravity slowed the clouds of hydrogen and helium, condensing the gases. As they grew smaller, they grew hotter and finally ignited, creating the first stars. Gravity then gathered the stars into galaxies. The first stars became matter factories, creating heavier elements.

Eight billion years ago our Milky Way galaxy formed, a second generation galaxy. Five billion years ago, our solar system formed, and our Earth took its place among the planets. Four billion years ago, amino acids, the basic building blocks for life as we know it, began to form. Three billion years ago, microbes began to develop and photosynthesis begins taking place, starting the process of adding to the atmosphere the oxygen we need to breathe. One and a half billion years ago, the first multi-cell life forms emerged. Five hundred million years ago, life suddenly burst forth in amazing variety and abundance so spectacular, scientists named it the Cambrian Explosion. Two hundred fifty million years ago, dinosaurs began to rule the Earth. Sixty five million years ago the dinosaurs died off in a mass extinction that allowed for the rapid development of mammals. Four million years ago the first hominids appeared. The evolutionary development of walking erect is of primal importance in our becoming human beings. It literally changed our perspective on the world. Standing erect, we see an entirely different world than when hunched over on all fours. Biologically, our walking erect also allowed for the development of the opposable thumb. With a thumb, we could carry a torch, wield a sword, use brush and pen, turn a door knob and work a remote control. Ten thousand years ago we saw the dawn of human civilization.(73)

All this great dance of creation took place, in part, for our development. We would not exist without it; we could not exist in any other universe. We are an integral part of the whole; the elements of the farthest star are also the elements that compose our own bodies. At any given point in the universe, all other points in the universe are moving away at the same rate of speed. In a sense, every place is the center of the universe!(74)

In the big bang of creation and the cosmic dance of the universe, we know there is something more. The big bang gave birth to space, time, energy and matter. But that is not all there is. The things we most value, most prize, in our lives are things other than these, not things at all, not material objects but relational subjects:

consciousness, truth, honesty and loyalty, respect, even love. Those elements that make our lives most real are not tangible, material objects, but all part of our subjective relationship with the world around us. Our emotions and our awareness are part of our essential being, and they are not at all composed of space, time, energy or matter. There is more to us, always more.

The universe began nearly as nothingness itself, all of existence fitting in less than a thimble. With the Big Bang, all creation came into being. The echoes of this shockwave still reverberate throughout the universe; it can be detected on all radio telescopes. It is as if God's first "Let there Be!" still vibrates in all that is.(75)

In the rush of that shock there was a struggle between matter and anti-matter, between being and not being. Matter barely won out; there is nearly as much anti-matter in the universe as there is matter. In our brief battle between our own being and our not being, in the microcosm of time that we call our life, this is a good thing to remember. The line between matter and anti-matter, between being and not being, is thin indeed.

As the universe expanded, creating space and time, it cooled and coalesced and there were the first clusters of the primal nascent stars that became furnace-factories, creating the stuff of which future generations of stars would be formed. The stars produced the material from which planets could form. The planets contain the environment and produce the atmosphere that enables life as we know it. And we are life that is graced with the awareness that we are alive, we are existence with the ability to realize our own existence. The universe itself evolved and may be seen as a living organism, of which we are the most miniscule of parts. Yet we are a part;

small as we are, we are a part of something big, bigger than our minds can understand or our imaginations dream.

Before there could be people, there had to be planets. Before there could be planets, there had to be stars. Before there could be stars, there had to be gaseous clouds, each being formed from that which went before, each giving itself to create that which was to follow. All creation, all of existence, all the cosmos, everything that is, that was, that will be, all that is, is in process, in evolution and procreation. The whole of creation is one of pilgrimage, one of constant growth and expansion.

What is more, the seed of creation is planted in each cell of the universe. The universe is holographic: each cell contains a replica of the whole, each cell is the universe in miniature. The discoveries and insights of Quantum physics have radically altered the way we look at the universe. It is a "both-and" creation rather than an "either-or".

For instance, light is both particle and wave, depending on how we construct the experiment. In the 1990's, experiments were carried out with atoms being individually fired through microscopic slits and observed. The results were striking; the atoms behaved as particles and as waves, depending on how the experiment was observed. The results even gave evidence that the atoms could somehow pass through two slits at once.(76)

Creation offers us a plethora of probabilities rather than the single focus of certainty. The results we find depend on what we look for and how we look for it. It is as if the universe were conscious, self-aware and aware and responsive to our questing. Indeed, it is as if the universe itself were on pilgrimage!(77)

Space itself, time itself, matter itself, all exist as part of the expression of the evolution of creation, of the being and becoming of existence. The dilemma of our existence, the dichotomy of our age, is that we know this, yet we deny it. We teach it in our classrooms, we study it in our libraries, we demonstrate it in laboratories and observatories, yet we refuse to acknowledge it in the living of our days.

We know we are made of the stuff of the stars, that the simple fact of our existence is dependent upon the entire flow of the cosmos, yet we live as if it were not so. We live our lives looking at the gutter instead of gazing at the stars. We consider ourselves masters of all creation instead of realizing that we are subjects of it. We look at all around us as objects in a collection rather than subjects in community with one another. We are so struck by the surface that we cannot see the depth and height and breadth of it all.

The truth is greater than we pretend it to be. We know it is, yet we continue to pretend. We are at once smaller than we pretend and greater than we imagine. The truth is that the mind cannot contain all that the heart can behold.

The tension between the pretended reality we attempt to control and the profound reality that envelopes us causes an internal disintegration within us and fractures our society around us.

Growing Discontent

It has happened to all of us. We are sitting at a traffic light, waiting for the signal to change. The timing always seems longer for the intersecting road, yet we wait. Then the turn lanes get to go, and we wait. Finally, we get the light. But before we can proceed with the light through the intersection, we have to wait for all the cars that are still turning left in front of us, after their light has changed: sometimes four, five or six cars, turning against the traffic and without the light.

Or we are moving through rush hour traffic, all lanes are jammed, and there are those few drivers who bounce from lane to lane like a pinball machine, pushing to make up just a few ticks of the clock. As a result of these and other erratic driving patterns, road rage seems to be of epidemic proportions. We'd all like to say to those running the red lights, those bouncing across lanes, those cutting in lines, "Your time is not worth my life!"

On an international scale, we see rogue nations and terrorism. North Korea launches missiles over Japanese territory. Civil war rages in Sudan, and thousands die in Darfur. Pakistan and India engage in nuclear brinksmanship. Al Qaida engages in holy war. Iran funds Hamas and Hezbollah, which kidnap three Israeli soldiers. Israel retaliates by kidnapping members of the Palestinian Parliament, bombing Beirut, killing hundreds, dislocating hundreds of thousands and causing a billion dollars in damage from bombings. Chechen rebels seize a school full of children. The terrorist attacks of September 11 are just the tip of the iceberg. From head butts on the field of the World Cup Soccer final to bombs in the London subways, there is an increase in violence everywhere.

Enron manipulates the energy market and laughs at wasting the life savings of the elderly. Worldcom manipulates their accounting records to inflate stock prices so the elite executives can gain greater bonuses. These executives eventually get caught, but their companies' employees and their pensions are often lost in the economic undertow. The question seems to be not what is morally exemplary or generally accepted accounting practices, but rather what can we get away with.

Our modern society is stressed, and it shows. There is a breakdown of morality, a breakdown of community, and an increase in violence on multiple levels, from road rage to terrorism and genocide. These are just gradations of scale, not inherent differences.

We have experienced an increase in the value of individual experience and expression that has led to an inflation of the ego and a splintering of the community. This has led to a loss of community consciousness and a loss of civility. A generation ago, our houses had front porches and sidewalks. We lived in neighborhoods and knew our neighbors, not just by name but actually knew them. Now our houses have small front stoops and large back decks or patios and high privacy fences. We don't want to know our neighbors and we don't want them looking in on us. No one just "drops by", better to make a phone call first. Our home is not just our castle, it is our fortress of solitude: we want to keep the world out.

Another example of the breakdown of community is the internet. The internet has added to the quality of life of everyone who has access. Communication between distant people is facilitated. It is now possible to do research into arcane pieces of information without traveling to a university's specialized library. News sources from around the world are available with just a few key strokes. At the same time, we can each spend our days or our nights in our own little rooms and never need to have real face to face conversations. Teens who would never talk with their parents have myspace websites sharing their deepest secrets with any stranger who gets their web address. We have conversations that are at once both intimate and anonymous. We don't know how to talk to people, only to machines. The internet can be a way to build a global consciousness of community, but it often is an extension of our individual egos.

Individuation is a good thing. Individuation is described as that process by which we discover our true selves, who we uniquely are.(78) We learn to distinguish ourselves from others and establish our personal identity. It is part of our maturation process. We learn to be who we are and relate with others as they are and recognize the boundary between our psyches. As Robert Frost would say, "Good fences make good neighbors." (79) We stand as individuals within a community of other individuals, recognizing that we are not simply projections of the community consciousness and realizing that they are not simply projections of our own psyche.

When individuation leads to alienating the self from the community, it has lost balance, lost equilibrium. When individuals become splintered from the community, we have moved from individualism to atomism, to psychotic narcissism. Psychotic narcissism results when we are too focused on our selves and our own pleasures, our own desires, even to the exclusion of the rights of others or the welfare of society. The world is not here to be an extension of my personal playground, not here to entertain or amuse me. It's not about me!

Our modern English word "idiot" is used to describe someone deficient in mental powers and development. The word comes from the ancient Greek and literally means "one's own."(80) An idiot, then, would be a person so stunted in their development that they are totally absorbed within themselves and lack the ability to relate with others or the world around them. Their psychotic narcissism has reached the level of a clinical obsession. This would explain a loss of civility, a loss of conversational abilities, and an increasing inability to relate with others. These extreme individuals do not see that the others around them are actually also living sentient beings of equal value and worth.

Martin Buber wrote of "I-thou" and "I-it" relationships and challenges us to know the difference and build appropriate relationships. I have "I-it" relationships with things and "I-thou" relationships with people, recognizing that others are of equal value and worth to myself, and I of equal value and worth to them. We relate with mutual respect and recognize that while we do have differences, we are also equals. Instead of using people and loving things, we love people and use things. Instead of treating the world as a collection of objects at our disposal, we view ourselves as subjects living in relationship with others.(81)

Anne Wilson Schaef is a contemporary writer and lecturer who speaks of "living in process."(82) This is a

74

way of living that engages life, shifting our focus from product to process so that we are aware and involved. It offers a way of doing rather than simply what is done, shifting our perception to the interconnectedness of life and helping us live from the inside as a subject and participant in community rather than controlling life from the outside as an object in a collection. It honors the challenges of life and reveals the mysteries of life.

According to Schaef, life is a process, we are a process and the whole universe is a process. She describes process as a way of doing rather than the thing that is done. Our challenge is to participate in the process of life that is going on all around us and within us, to celebrate the mystery of life rather than attempt to master the control of it.

In many instances and many observations, we see that what we are doing and how we are living is not working. Frustrations are vented in our daily commutes and our athletic fields, in the executive offices of our largest corporations and our own personal experiences. With examples from business, sports, the internet, psychology and philosophy, we see the disintegration of self and society. We are hectic but not happy, frantic and not fulfilled, busy yet bored. Our houses are filled and our hearts are empty. There must be a better way!

From Our Ancient Past, A New Beginning

We are born learning from our elders. Our parents nurture us and become unconscious guides for our lives. Our siblings play with us, tease and torment us, wrestle with us and establish relationships that linger within us. Our grandparents, aunts and uncles, all imprint themselves upon us in ways we can never fully know. Grandparents relate with their grandchildren in ways that parents cannot relate with their children. In school, we study the lives of those past, in our history, our language, our literature. We are born learning from our elders.

In the anatomy of our brain we have the limbic system, that regulates our autonomic nervous system and our emotions. It is vital to our health, as it controls body temperature, pulse and breathing, the things we do without thinking. And certainly we are known to act upon our emotions without thinking them through! The limbic system governs that most primitive part of our human development. It might be called, "the elder within."(83)

Even our cells have memory. Cell memory improves the ability of cells to react to stimuli and respond to their environment. People who have been transplant patients, especially heart transplants, recall how their tastes preferences have changed after such transformative surgery. These patients tend to develop new tastes and preferences similar to those of the donor. The cells in the organ retain a memory from the donor and transfer it to the recipient.(84)

Jung discusses the collective subconscious, elements of our subconsciousness that are common to all humans, what he calls our "racial memory" but would more accurately be called "species memory." There is a part of us that remembers the past, even the deep primeval past. It is the elder within that remembers the ways of the ancients, our ancestors, ways we moderns have forgotten. We have forgotten them, but they are still a part of us, still our ways as well.(85)

The ancient Celts were primitives and aborigines and shared much in common anthropologically with other aborigines: a closeness with the created world, a pervasive sense of the sacredness of all life. The Celts also had some unique gifts as a people, as all aboriginal groups had distinct traits. These ancient Celts, and especially the Christian Celts, our spiritual elders, have much to teach us. The characteristics of Celtic Christdian spirituality not only tell us of a people from long ago, they can remind us of who we are. From our ancient past, we may gain a new beginning.(86)

The Celts had a love of and respect for their physical environment. They lived "at one with" their world rather than apart from it. There was a oneness with nature. What is more, they viewed all creation as holy, every life as sacred, each moment as divine. Indeed, they experienced creation as the "first scripture." The written words of the text came secondarily. The first scripture, first canon, was the living text of creation itself. To read creation was to read the Creator.

With the created order came an appreciation of time as part of the sacred reality, already blessed by overflowing compassion. If all things are holy and every place divine, then time must also be sacred. The passage of time and the process of human aging are all part of the divine reality within which we live. Aging is not a thing to be avoided, denied or hidden. Rather, it is to be cherished, to be celebrated, to be enjoyed. Life is good and living it is our calling and our responsibility. Aging means we have been blessed with more life to live, and gained the wisdom of our years.

There was an appreciation of the ordinary in life. Within the ordinary is hidden the extraordinary and within the mundane we find the divine. Each moment is filled with the fullness of eternity, each object a wonder, each event a miracle. Life is not a problem to be solved but a miracle to be cherished. We stand amazed, filled with awe and wonder, at the abundance of divine goodness that is all around us, so extravagant that the extraordinary is made to appear but ordinary. All life is sacred festival, meant to be enjoyed fully, shared generously, cherished gently.

With this came an appreciation of the cycles of the world and the seasons of life. There's a story of God granting the Irish to live in a tropical paradise, and they graciously decline, confessing that they prefer the turning of the seasons of the year. Fall to Winter, Winter to Spring, Spring to Summer, Summer back to Fall, is all part of God's great design for creation.(87) Likewise, the growth of baby to child, child to youth, youth to adult, adult to elder, is all part of the great design of the gift of life. Our role is to enjoy each phase, celebrate each step, cherish each part.

79

With the love and appreciation of nature came a longing for silence and solitude, to be at one with one's own self as well as at one with the world around us, to look within us as well as around us. If we don't know our own souls, how can we know our world? If the divine is indeed all around us, even within us, how can we not attend to that divine presence with our own presence?

The love of silence and solitude and the appreciation of cycles and seasons led to a balancing of solitude with community. The Celts longed for silence, and they also very much enjoyed being with one another. Celtic society did not build large cities, but they did dot the landscape with villages, clusters of communities being at one with themselves, at one with the world around them and at one with each other. Hospitality was not only an honored duty, it was a holy privilege. Hosts prided themselves on being generous and gracious to their guests. Dancing, music, story-telling were all part of Celtic society that was very much cherished, honored and respected. One of their sayings demonstrates this: "Never trust a warrior who cannot sing."(88) It was as manly to sing as to swing a sword. To be mature is to be complete, to be balanced, and this is always a "both –and," not an "either-or." We cannot fully be in community if we do not also have our solitude. We cannot truly be in solitude if we do not also have our community. Life has a balance and a rhythm to it, and we are invited to join in the dance.

All life is sacred and every place holy, yet there are special times and places where the barrier between physical and spiritual, between ordinary and divine, between this world and the next world, the unseen or spiritual world, seem so thin as to be permeable. These times and places when the physical seemed filled with the spiritual, the mundane radiant with the divine, the ordinary bursting with the sacred, were called "thin times" and "thin places" because the veil separating the two realms seemed so thin. One might slip imperceptibly from one side to the other. These were sacred times and places, and sometimes scary ones as well. The holy is always other, the divine presence always transcendent as well as immanent. Thin times and places were held in special regard and with special respect.

The Celtic experience and expression of life is one of relationship and flow, of being at one with one's self and with the process, present and participating. As there are seasons of nature, there are seasons of life and seasons of the emotions. There is an ebb and flow to the tide, a changing of the wind, and a recognition of the importance of being honest and open in our grieving and spontaneous in our humor. When they were saddened, the expressed those depths of grief. When they were glad, they rejoiced in it. They believed in living the moment they had to live. Their grief was real and their joy was full. They were free to feel what they felt, think what they thought, and were honest and open in their emotions and opinions. It was all part of being real and being alive, living fully in the present moment.

With community comes conviviality. Community means to live in common with others: not just strangers who live beside one another, but genuine neighbors, freeholders who stand beside one another. When we live in genuine community, knowing those with whom we live, sharing life together and caring about one another, then we also become truly convivial, living life together as a feast. We are friends and not simply strangers who live near one another. We are not mere passengers on the commute of blurring rush of our days, but pilgrims along the way celebrating the bounty of the feast of life.

With the love and respect of the created order, the appreciation and honoring of time, the celebration of seasons and passages, rhythms and balances of life, came a love of learning. There is so much of life to enjoy and experience, so much to participate in, that there is also so much learn. Beyond every leaf is a tree, within every seed is a plant. Behind every answer lies another question. There is always more to learn! This was especially inherited from the Druid culture in the pagan Celts. The Druids were the judges, philosophers, teachers and healers of Celtic culture. Their apprenticeship might last twenty years and depended heavily on memorization, for the Druids regarded their language as too sacred to be written. The Druids could read and write Latin, but would not write their own language.(89)

The Celts had a native desire for learning that did not exist on the continent. After the collapse of the Roman empire, the next great center of learning was on the island of Ireland, and Gaelic replaced Latin as the language most widely used.(90) St. Patrick claimed Christ as his druid.(91) St. Columba was born a prince, studied as a druid and trained to be priest. The three were seen as complimentary, not contradictory, each one adding to the others.(92)

If we are open to appreciate all that is around us, open to enjoy the beauty and wonder in each passing moment, open to participating in the fullness of life in this verdant garden paradise, then we are also open to all the mysteries yet to be revealed, wisdom yet to be passed on. Learning becomes a natural part of living.

In our relationships, there are special relationships. Among our friends, there are best friends. In the bonds of community, there are strong bonds. There is great value in kinship relationships, those with whom through time or experience we have developed a special closeness, a sense of comradeship. In these strong and intimate relationships, there are still those which are unique, which hold us dearer. Celtic Christians had a unique relationship of spiritual friends, of soul friends, "Anam Chara."(93) These relationships were holy and precious gifts. A soul friend was one you bared your soul to, you shared your heart with, one from whom no secrets were kept. A soul friend kept the other honest, growing in their life and going on their way. St. Brigit wrote, "A soul without a friend is like a body without a head."(94) Attempting to live the fullness of life without a soul friend would be like a surgeon operating on himself, an attorney defending herself. Not only was it unadvisable, in the end it would prove impossible. A body without a head has no direction, no sense, no sight. A body without a head is lost, and a soul without a friend is lost indeed.

Last of all, the Celts had a yearning to travel and to explore the unknown. As a people, the Celts are generally believed to have originated in central Europe and spread out from there. But even these first Celts had to have come from someplace. Some have speculated that their origin was on the steppes of eastern Europe. Some have speculated perhaps from northern India. From their beginning, it seems the Celts have been wandering. From their central European base, they spread south into Italy, east into Turkey, west into France and Spain, north to Ireland and Scotland. When the Romans came, the Celts were left with the fringes of Europe: the peninsulas of

Gallicia in Spain, Brittany in France, Cornwall and Wales in England, and the northern reaches of Scotland, Ireland and the Isle of Man, each one never fully subdued by the Romans and now offering us the richest stores of Celtic treasure.

The Celts were born to wander. As they settled, their traveling turned to conquering, but still they explored. When they became Christian, their conquering changed to pilgrimage, yet they explored. Monks traveled from the green wilderness of Ireland to the desert wilderness of Egypt, Palestine and Syria. Celtic monks turned Christian missionaries in re-converting the continent to their faith. Pilgrims set off in ships with no oars, determined to let the wind of the spirit direct them. St. Brendan explored the North Atlantic. St. Columbanus walked throughout Europe, founding communities and then traveling on. The Celts were born to wander; but, as Tolkein says, not all who wander are lost.

For the Celts, life was a pilgrimage and pilgrimage was their life. It is about the journey not the destination, the process not the product. Life is about being on the way and enjoying the trip, participating fully in each passing moment and finding eternity revealed there in all its fullness. Life is about experiencing not accumulating, about sharing not hoarding, about learning not acquiring.

Life is a pilgrimage from the place of our birthing to the place of our rising. Not those who wander are lost, but those who refuse to wander and who will not wonder. We are born to be pilgrims and to be on pilgrimage. Like the Peregrine that is our namesake, we are born for the flight and not the nesting.

Life as Pilgrimage

Early in the morning the Christian Celts of the Hebrides would rise from their sleep and walk out of their homesteads to a remote place, distant from hearth and home yet where all their world could be seen. There in that remote quietness, they would chant their morning prayers, calling for divine blessing upon all the world around them, from hearth to horizon, and upon all whom they knew and loved, both kith and kin. They sought to see the sacredness of all creation, hidden and revealed, in and through their daily lives.

If life is a pilgrimage and we are pilgrims, that makes a statement about how we see ourselves and the world we live in, how we live our daily lives. We need a paradigm of pilgrimage as the path for our personal lives - a way that is personal but not individual, that is relational and subjective rather than objective, that focuses on the quality of life rather than quantifying life.

In the morning when I rise, I go to a quiet room where I can face the rising of the sun. Standing there in the silence, I offer my own morning prayer, one I learned from the Celtic Christians. "Deep Peace of the blowing wind to you," I say, turning and stretching my torso around to my right. "Deep Peace of the flowing wave to you," I say, turning and stretching my torso around to my left. "Deep Peace of the quiet earth to you," I say, bending and stretching from my waist to touch the floor beneath my feet. "Deep Peace of the shining star to you," I say, reaching and stretching up with my arms, spreading toward the heavens. "Deep Peace of the Son of Peace to you," I say, reaching and stretching my arm down and out to all around me. "Deep Peace of the Son of Peace," I repeat, bringing my arms up and folding them over my heart.

This "Prayer of Deep Peace" encircles all of creation, the whole of the cosmos. It unites the four directions of East and West, North and South. It joins together the four elements envisioned by the ancients, air and water, earth and fire. It moves my body to form a Celtic Cross: my arms the circle, my torso the crux. It ends with my hands folded around me, in the form of medieval prayer. It is a uniting of my present day with an ancient age, of my spirit with those who have gone before me. It is a way to open me, body and soul, to the gift of this new day.

Then I am ready to sit, to breathe, to listen, to pray, to be in the quiet of the divine presence, that still small voice. Not a prayer of speaking but a prayer of listening. Not a prayer of acting but a prayer of waiting. Not a prayer of doing but a prayer of being. I have a timer set for twenty minutes. I give these minutes as a gift from my day to the whole of eternity.

Pilgrims are those who sense the sacred in their life, and seek to strengthen its hold on their lives. Pilgrims are those who have a hunger in their hearts that is not satisfied with tangible things, with superficial realities. Subaru has an ad that says, "Those who say 'Getting there is half the fun' only got half way there." Celtic pilgrims say "Getting there" is the whole point; life is in the "getting there," not in the arriving. Life is found in the process, not in the arriving. Life is a journey, and the purpose of life is not to "get there" but to enjoy the journey!

Pilgrims are those who are on pilgrimage, who see their life as a pilgrimage. In days of old, pilgrimage was always on foot. Travel was slow, tedious, even dangerous. A lack of creature comfort was seen as adding to the sense and experience of pilgrimage. Today we have made necessities of our luxuries. We hurry to every appointment, we worry when we're forced to wait, forced to stand in line, forced to "take the time." We don't want to waste time, we want to make time.

We need to cherish time, to enjoy time, to celebrate time. Each moment of our lives stands ready to reveal the mysteries of eternity, if we are willing to see. Pilgrims, being people on a holy journey, know that each moment of the journey and each stop along the way is holy. If the journey is holy, then the times and places of the journey are holy. How different would our lives be if we approached each day as a revealing of the divine presence? How different would be the travels and commutes of our daily lives if we saw in each place a revealing of the sacred? Suddenly each day becomes divine and each place becomes sacred.

When we drive our cars, we speed past sights without seeing them. Walking allows us to be at one with our environment, to participate in it rather than simply observe it. Walking allows us to slow ourselves down. A leisurely walk at a relaxed pace allows me to more fully be part of the world around me. I can take long, slow, deep breaths. I can breathe the air, feel the breeze, hear the sounds, see the sights. It helps me to clear my mind and helps me relax. Our ancient ancestors populated the world by walking, pilgrims of old made holy journeys by walking; is it any wonder that walking is so good for our souls?

Relax, have fun, enjoy life, and enjoy the journey! Take the time to soak in the richness, the fullness of each passing moment. We have it only for an instant, yet it comes to us from the dawn of time and calls to us from the echoes of eternity.

Celtic pilgrims celebrated the sacredness of all life and respected every calling as divine. They saw the holy infused in all of creation, both natural and human. This is a spirituality that is free from religious structure, a quest for meaning that is independent of doctrine or dogma, a mystical experience in the truest sense of the word rather than simply a religious one. A mystical experience is an immediate personal encounter with the divine, a sense of being at one with the unity of the cosmos, an experience that strikes at the root of our being, a presence that for us makes plain our own purpose in life.

All the world's religions began with the mystic experience, in the human encounter with the Divine Other. The mystic, who is so consumed and transformed by the experience, naturally attracts followers who see the difference and desire it in their own lives. Spiritual traditions and practices develop around the mystic and this mystical experience, disciplines that are designed to lead practitioners to the experience itself. Around these spiritual traditions accrue religious institutions, intended to protect this mystical experience and provide these spiritual traditions for others. Eventually, the religious institutions harden and the spiritual traditions deaden and the original mystical experience, so treasured, is lost. We need to capture it again, we need to remember we are pilgrims, who are on the way. Pilgrims are those who travel light, who breathe easy and who trust the road before them.

Pilgrims can't be bogged down by where they've been, they can't be weighed down by their past burdens. Pilgrims don't borrow worries from the future nor grief or guilt from the past. The day is sufficient unto itself. Pilgrims live life one day at a time, and therefore focus on the fullness of life that is within that day and revealed in the surroundings before them. Traveling light means we carry only what we need, and we keep our needs at a minimum. Traveling light is the opposite of our society's acquisitive nature, hoarding and accumulating. Traveling light means we hold things lightly, gently, openly, graciously. We desire freedom for ourselves and hence for all things and all others. Traveling light means we are fully present to the present moment. It also means we keep an eye on the horizon, celebrating where we are and remembering where we are bound. We don't get attached in our vanity to the good times, nor do we get attached in our remorse to the bad times. Things happen. Life has its ebb and flow, its high and low. In all things, we remember the philosopher's dictum, "This, too, shall pass." Pilgrims travel light: a lightness of burdens, of worries and concerns, a lightness from attachments, a lightness of heart.

Julian of Norwich, a mystic from 14th century England, had this experience. She was an anonymous woman living during a time of civil war and the Black Plague, when a third of the population was wiped out. She was homeless and took her refuge in a lean-to shanty outside of Norwich Cathedral. She suffered a high fever and nearly died. With the fever came visions, visions she described as revelations of divine love. In all this outer chaos and inner turmoil, she knew in the depths of her being, that "all shall be well and all shall be well and all manner of things shall be well."(95)

Pilgrims breathe easy. Breathe long, slow, deep steady breaths. Breathe in and feel the rush of air entering the lungs, fresh and clean. Hold that breath, let it linger in the lungs, feel its fullness filling your whole person. Draw out all that this breath, this moment, has to offer. Then slowly, gently, lovingly, release the air back into the universe. Let go of all that is stale, all that is used, old, dead, in your life. Breathe out slowly and completely. Let your lungs remind you what it feels like to be empty. Remember that for a vessel to be filled, it must first be emptied. Then breathe in again, long, slow, deep and steady. Feel your lungs filled again, your life renewed again, all things made new again.

With each breath, we live; with each breath, we pray. To pray is to breathe and to breathe is to pray. Each breath reminds us of the giftedness of life, reminds us to cherish life and hold it gently. Each breath reminds us of the sacredness of life; each breath shares in the divine presence, around and now within us. Each breath reminds us we are pilgrims. We breathe in particles from the dawn of time, elements from the beginning of creation. Every breath includes molecules that had their birth in the stars. Each time we exhale, we exchange pieces of our own DNA, molecular scraps from our lungs and linings that contain our deepest secrets, keys to our uniqueness. Our breathing makes us one with the cosmos.

The atmosphere breathes in the circuits of the air. Nature breathes in the passing of the seasons. The oceans breathe in the flow of tides and streams. The world breathes in the patterns of climate and weather. The planet breathes earthquakes and eruptions. All creation is alive with the glory of God and we are at one with the fullness of life, aware of the sacredness of each breath, experiencing divinity in each breath. As pilgrims, we breathe easily.

The Russian classic, The Way of the Pilgrim includes a pattern that connects our breath and our prayer, our body and our soul. A pilgrim sought out a hermit for direction in finding the presence of God in his life. The hermit told him to pray the Jesus prayer a hundred times a day: "Lord Jesus Christ, son of God, have mercy on me, a sinner." The pilgrim worked to achieve this, counting carefully each time he prayed. When he attained one hundred times a day, he returned to the hermit. "Now pray it a thousand times a day." Again the pilgrim worked to achieve this new regimen. Upon completing the task, he again returned to the hermit. "Now ten thousand times." The pilgrim dutifully developed this greater discipline. Finally, he returned to the hermit. "What have you learned?" asked the hermit. "That God is as near as my next breath, that all the world is filled with God's presence." So it is with every pilgrim who has learned to breathe easily.(96)

Pilgrims trust the road they are on. Pilgrims are "on the way" rather than "in the way." Travelers are frequently caught being "in the way" of others. Who has not been trapped waiting in line, waiting behind others or waiting for others? We are ahead or we are behind, but we never seem to be together. Pilgrims are on the way, and pilgrims are with others, in relationship. Pilgrims are fully present in the present moment, yet also with an eye to the horizon. The place we are, we want to be aware of, to experience and to understand. But the place we are, wherever it is, however wonderful it may be, is not our destination; we are "on the way."

Because pilgrims live in relationship with others, as subjects in a community rather than objects in a collection, they trust the dynamics of that living relationship, a relationship that has a life of its own. Pilgrims live in inter-dependence. A relationship of dependence denotes immaturity and inferiority. A relationship of independence is not one of true maturity, but rather a false superiority. The pilgrim realizes that all of life is integrated in a web of relationship, therefore the appropriate relationship is one of inter-dependence, a relationship between equals, with mutual trust and respect for one another.

The pilgrim realizes there are many roads, each road unique with its own gifts and graces and fraught with its own fears and frailties. Yet each road leads to the one goal. There are many paths, but one Center. The point is not to get all pilgrims to travel the same path, but rather to help each one along their own way. Any search for truth, any desire for meaning or purpose in life, if it is pursued sincerely, will lead inevitably and inexorably to the divine truth. All we need do is pursue our own path; in the end, we will all be one with the One.

Pilgrims travel light, breathe easily and trust their path. Pilgrims are not attached to institutions or traditions, but seek the experience of divinity itself, the awareness of it in their days and the understanding of it for their lives. As the Peregrine Falcon, pilgrims live for the pursuit.

Prayers for the Pilgrimage

The Celtic Christians enjoyed a spirituality that was both deep and practical. They had prayers for every experience of life and for the events of their daily routine: prayers for rising in the morning and preparing for the day, for building the fire and setting the table, for leaving the house and doing the chores, for cleaning and cooking, for fishing and farming. They would say the prayers softly, murmuring them repeatedly throughout the day. In doing this, each act was made holy and all time made sacred, and the one praying was made aware of the divine presence that surrounded and accompanied them.

A story is told of a mother scolding her children for not saying their prayers as they did their chores, "The birds fly above us for the glory of God, the clouds are in the sky for the glory of God, the waves lap the shore for the glory of God, the fish leaps in the sea for the glory of God, the flowers bloom on the hills for the glory of God, the trees spread their branches for the glory of God, all creation rejoices for the glory of God, and will my own children be silent?"(97) Certainly, a sense of the fullness of life in each present moment was the intended expectation for these Christian Celts.

Some samples of their prayers are given below. Saying them may serve to remind us of the sacredness of each moment or inspire us to compose some prayers of our own. Some ancient and some modern, these prayers all reflect the sense of the divine presence on our daily path, making each day holy and each act sacred. As we open ourselves to experience fully all that each moment holds for us and offers to us, we realize the beauty and wonder that is always all about us. We make ourselves to be pilgrims and our life to be a pilgrimage.

Petition
"Be thou a smooth way before me, be thou a guiding
    star above me,
Be thou a keen eye behind me, this day, this night, for
    ever.
If only thou, O God of life, be at peace with me, be
    my support,
Be to me as a star, be to me as a helm,
From my lying down in peace to my rising anew."(98)

Journey Blessing
"Bless to me, O God, the earth beneath my foot,
Bless to me, O God, the path whereon I go;
Bless to me, O God, the thing of my desire;
Thou evermore of evermore, bless thou to me my rest.
Bless to me the thing whereon is set my mind,
Bless to me the thing whereon is set my love;
Bless to me the thing whereon is set my hope;
O thou King of kings, bless thou to me mine
    eye!"(99)

The Pilgrim's Aiding
"God be with thee in every pass, Jesus be with thee on
    every hill,
Spirit be with thee on every stream, headland and
    ridge and lawn;
Each sea and land, each moor and meadow, each
    lying down, each rising up,
In the trough of the waves, on the crest of the billows,
Each step of the journey thou goest."(100)

"As Thou wast before at my life's beginning,
Be Thou so again at my journey's end.
As Thou wast besides at my soul's shaping,
Father, be Thou too at my journey's close.
Be with me at each time, lying down and arising,
Be with me in sleep companioned by dear ones.
Be with me a-watching each evening and morning,
And allure me home to the land of the saints."(101)

"God before me, God behind me, God above me, God
    beneath me.
I on your path O God, You, O God, on my way.
In the twistings of the road, In the currents of the river
Be with me by day, Be with me by night, Be with me
    by day and by night."(102)

"Bless to me O God the earth beneath my feet.
Bless to me O God the path on which I go.
Bless to me O God the people whom I meet.
O God of all gods bless to me my life."(103)

The Path
"God bless the path on which you go, God bless the
 earth beneath your feet,
God bless your destination.
God be a smooth way before you, a guiding star
 above you,
A keen eye behind you, this day, this night, and
 forever.
God be with you whatever you pass, Jesus be with
 you whatever you climb,
Spirit be with you wherever you stay.
God be with you at each stop and each sea, at each
 lying down and each rising up,
In the trough of the waves, on the crest of the billows,
Each step of the journey you take."(104)

Circuit
"I make my circuit in the fellowship of my God
On the machair, in the meadow, on the cold heathery
 hill,
On the corner in the open, on the chill windy dock,
To the noise of drills blasting, to the sound of children
 asking.
I make my circuit in the fellowship of my God
In city street or on spring-turfed hill, in shop-floor
 room or at office desk.
God has no favorite places. There are no special
 things.
All are God's and all is sacred.
I tread each day, in light or dark, in the fellowship of
 my God.

Be the sacred Three of glory interwoven with our
lives
Until the Man who walks it with us leads us home,
through death to life."(105)

All Shall be Well
"For the greening of trees and the gentling of friends,
we thank you, God.
For the brightness of field and the warmth of the sun,
we thank you, God.
For work to be done and laughter to share we thank
you, God.
We thank you, and know that through struggle and
pain,
In the slippery path of new birth, hope will be born
and all shall be well."(106)

Bless to Us, O God
"Bless to us, O God, the doors we open,
The thresholds we cross, the roads that lie before us,
Go with us as we go and welcome us home."(107)

As You Were
"As you were in the ebb and flow, as the beginning
becomes the ending,
And the ending a new beginning, be with us, ever-
present God."(108)

97

Wherever We Go

"Wherever we go, may the joy of God the gracious be
with us.

Wherever we go, may the face of Christ the kindly be
with us.

Wherever we go, may the compassing of the Spirit of
grace be with us.

Wherever we go, may the compassing of the Spirit of
grace be with us.

Wherever we go, the presence of the Trinity around us
to bless and to keep us."(109)

The Way of the Pilgrim

If life is meant to be a pilgrimage, a search for meaning and quest for purpose, how would that be different from the life we are typically leading? If life is a pilgrimage, how do we live as pilgrims? If life is a quest for purpose rather than an acquisition of possessions, how do we pursue that quest? If life is a search for depth meaning rather than a striving for wealth of material, how would that search be different? How do we live a life of pilgrimage?

As the Celts had prayers for each act in their daily lives and rituals for the tasks they performed, from smooring the fire to milking the cow, from churning the butter to crossing the threshold, from sweeping the mantle to plowing the field, so the Pilgrim has prayers and rituals for use throughout the day in order to be mindful of the blessedness of each passing moment and the eternity that is revealed. The elements of creation were the substance of eternity; earth, air, water and fire were divine offerings that filled with world with divine presence and purpose. The Pilgrim is mindful of this.

The Pilgrim awakens in the morning. Lying in bed, the Pilgrim remains quiet, waking slowly into the morning of a new day, a new act of creation. With eyes still closed, the Pilgrim draws in a long, slow, deep breath. Giving thanks for the freshness that fills his lungs, the Pilgrim holds that breath. Cherishing the act of breathing and the gift of life, the Pilgrim feels her lungs that are now full with the freshness, the vigor, of this new day. Then slowly, gently, lovingly, the Pilgrim relaxes his lungs, breathes out and releases all the staleness that has accumulated during the night's sleep.

Continuing to breathe long, slow, deep, steady breaths, the Pilgrim stretches while still reclining in bed. Stretching arms and legs, wiggling fingers and toes, the Pilgrim feels what it feels like to be alive. With his body outstretched, the Pilgrim forms a circle with her arms and legs, gently stretching and slowly wakening his body before rising, like a cat stretches upon waking.

"Circle me, Lord: keep peace within, keep trial
    without;
Circle me, Lord: keep hope within, keep despair
    without;
Circle me, Lord: keep love within, keep hate without;
Circle me, Lord: keep joy within, keep despair
    without." (110)
The Pilgrim awakens for the journey of this new day.

Upon rising, the Pilgrim continues to loosen limbs and stretch muscles. Mindful that her self is a whole: mind, body and soul, the Pilgrim loosens his body to open her soul, the Pilgrim stretches his muscles to open her mind.

Showering, the Pilgrim give thanks for the gift of water, such a crucial element for life to exist. Remembering baptism in the act of bathing, the Pilgrim cleans the spirit as well as the flesh. Each act of preparing for the day is an opportunity to practice mindfulness, to prepare oneself to fully participate in each act of the day as it unfolds: shaving, brushing and flossing teeth, brushing and combing hair, putting on make-up. Putting on glasses or contact lenses is a reminder of the prayer of

Richard of Chichester, made popular in the musical "Godspell:" "see thee more clearly, love thee more dearly, follow thee more nearly, day by day." (111)

Dressing continues the discipline of directing and focusing life. The Pilgrim's loins are girded with truth, heart is covered with righteousness, feet with peace, arms with faith, head with wholeness and words are seasoned with goodness. (112) Eating breakfast is not a hurried affair, but an opportunity to give thanks for the bounty of the earth, "taste and see that the Lord is good." (113)

The commute to work is part of the pilgrimage of life, an outer journey with an inner purpose. It is entered into carefully and advisedly, as the Pilgrim becomes part of the flow of the traffic, part of the web of life. Knowing that others are also on the journey, he makes room for them in the lane, welcoming companions along the way. The Pilgrim is a careful and courteous driver and a cheerful passenger. Sharing with others in time and space is how she builds community, however transient that community may be. The Pilgrim knows life is a balance: between solitude and community, between stillness and the dance, between giving and receiving.

Life is a symphony, and each pilgrim an instrument in the orchestra. They play in harmony with one another, sharing and cooperating rather than competing, and so making music suitable for the dance of life. Pilgrims enjoy the give and take of life, the ebb and flow. They allow space for one another and welcome others along the way. Pilgrims give room for merging traffic, hold doors on crowded elevators, and find ways to give time and space for one another. Time and space are sacred objects, and sharing them is ritual practice.

The Pilgrim goes through the day with this attitude of openness and welcome toward others, mindful of each moment and attentive to each detail. The Pilgrim is a participant in the events of the day, not an observer, sharing in the events rather than manipulating either the occasions or the others involved. Honest and open with others and true to her own sense of call, his own inner destiny, the Pilgrim lives a life of pilgrimage.

At the end of the day, the Pilgrim reviews the day that is past. Knowing that all time is thin time and all places are thin places, that the consciousness of the cosmos is revealed in each passing moment, the Pilgrim carefully examines the events that he has lived, patiently remembers each person she has met that day. Each event is a sacred event, each person is a holy person. The Pilgrim also reviews his own life, lived out in the events of the day and with the people of the day, for the Pilgrim is one of those persons who is holy. He asks himself how he offered the divine to others, she asks herself how her presence was a blessing in the moments of the day, making the moments to be holy moments and sharing in the sacredness of the day.

Having lived the day to the full, having been fully present to the divine presence that is in each passing present moment, the Pilgrim is ready to rest at the end of the day. Because he has lived fully, his body is ready to relax. Because she has given freely and received abundantly, her spirit is at peace and she can sleep. It will not be a restless night or a tormented sleep; it will be a sleep of peace and a night of resting in the eternity that has been lived within.

The way of the Pilgrim is a path of relaxed attention, of calm assurance and of gracious openness. It is part of the path of eternity, the way that is from of old. It is willing to receive, knowing that all gifts are filled with the divine and flow from the divine. It is willing to give, knowing that the source of unlimited abundance flows through his gift, the purpose of eternity is at work through her generosity.

Because life itself is a pilgrimage, that pilgrimage cannot end as long as the Pilgrim lives. Each day is another step along the way, another lesson to be learned, another gift to be shared. Life is a pilgrimage, from the place of our birthing to the place of our rising. We are all pilgrims, and each of our lives a pilgrimage. The pilgrimage is our purpose and our life is our path. We continue on our way, each day filled with purpose and flowing with purpose, making for a wealth of meaning.

The Flight of the Peregrine

A Peregrine falcon soars high overhead, its fleeting shadow invisible amongst the tall prairie grasses, wafting in the wind. With eyes as piercing as they appear, it surveys its surroundings. It seeks not to be an individual, standing out from its surroundings, but rather to be at one with them, its identity blended with its environment. It is neither lost nor isolated. The falcon is fully aware of all it experiences, and it experiences all that is around it, aware of and at one with its environment.

The Peregrine is born to hunt, born to pursue; it is born with a hunger inside that will not be satisfied only with outer realities. The Peregrine is born for flight and for the hunt, its hunt and its flight are one. The Peregrine is one with its flight, one with its world and one with its pilgrimage. It feeds on its environment and is nurtured and sustained by it, but the hunt and the flight continue. It is not enough to eat and be done; the Peregrine does not live to eat, it lives to hunt and for the flight.

Surveying the whole of the world before it, the Peregrine's vision scans the horizon and studies the detail. With such great vision, it can see into the depths of the world around it. Then with a fierce focus, the Peregrine dives down, seeing only its quarry. Swooping abruptly heavenward again, the meal is consumed in flight. Nothing interferes with the flight; the meal sustains it. It eats, but it is not filled. It lives for the flight, not the food.

The hunger of the Peregrine is not a thing to be satisfied; it is part of who and what the Peregrine is. A falcon in flight is a thing of wonder and beauty, filled with power and grace. It fulfills that for which it was made. The Peregrine is not made for the roost or the nest, it is not born for resting but for flight. The Peregrine lives for the flight and the seeking. It pierces its world with its penetrating eye, to behold that which lies within and beneath, above and beyond, the meaning in the matter around it.

Flying from nesting to resting, the Peregrine is born for perpetual flight, perpetual pilgrimage. Its home is the hunt, its place the pilgrimage, its joy the journey, its destination the road itself.

The Peregrine is a wanderer, a pilgrim. Not all who wander do so aimlessly, not all who wander are lost. Pilgrims are those on pilgrimage, their life is to be on the way and in process - always traveling, never arriving. They are consumed and compelled by an inner fire, a guiding light that both leads them and calls them. It leads them from within and pushes them. It calls them from ahead and pulls at them. They are hunters who are born for the hunt. Obtaining the prey is not enough, they are not satisfied except by the hunt itself.

The Celtic Christians saw themselves as pilgrims, peregrines, and their lives as a pilgrimage, peregrinatio. Each day was a step on the way. Life is not about arriving at the destination, about achievement, accomplishment or acquisition. Life is about the journey, the pilgrimage: being on the way, aware of the way and at one with the way, just as the Peregrine falcon. Life is a journey from the place of our birthing to the place of our rising, and each day a holy celebration of this sacred calling.

We, too, are peregrines - pilgrims, always on pilgrimage, on the way, never arriving. Like the Peregrine, we are born to hunt, to seek out meaning and purpose, richness and fullness, in the midst of life, beneath its surface, above its ordinariness, beyond its mundane. We wander and we wonder, we seek, study, inquire. We fly as Peregrines over the plains of our existence, hunting out those flashes of inspiration, those instances of experience that can satisfy the hunger of our hearts and longing of our soul.

We are not content with the material contents of our lives, nor are we meant to be. We are more about becoming than we are about being, and more about being than we are about doing. There is always something more, something beyond. Our destiny is in our desiring, not our destination! Like the Peregrine, we are created for the calling not the resting, born for the quest and the journey. Our fulfillment is always "on the way."

Life is a pilgrimage from the place of our birthing to the place of our rising. We are born for the journey, called for the quest. It is our destiny to be "on the way." And we are the pilgrims, Peregrines, born to be on the path rather than at the place, born to be in flight and on the hunt, pilgrims born for the pilgrimage. May we enjoy the journey, and find our life's fulfillment in the flight of the Peregrine.

Notes

1. Madeline Dunfy, <u>The Peregrine's Journey.</u> (Millbrook).
2. Attributed to Sigmund Freud on a variety of web sites, including http://www.cybernation.com/victory/quotations/directory.html, and http://www.quotationsbook.com/.
3. Phillip J. Newell, <u>One Foot in Heaven</u> (Paulist Press, 1999), chapter 7, "Death and Return", pp. 81-89. Also see Esther de Waal's <u>The Celtic Way of Prayer</u> (Doubleday, 1997), pp. 3f.
4. The information and inspiration for this section comes from Madeline Dunfy's <u>The Peregrine's Journey,</u> cited above, and from Alan Tennant's <u>On the Wing</u> (Knopf, 2004).
5. See Dunfy and Tennant.
6. See Dunfy and Tennant.
7. Victor Turner, <u>The Ritual Process</u> (Hawthorne, 1995).
8. Ibid.
9. Thomas Hobbes, <u>Leviathan</u> (Penguin Classics, 1982) especially chapter 13, "On the Natural Condition of Mankind". Originally published in 1651.
10. Jean Jacques Rousseau, <u>The Social Contract</u> (Penguin Classics, 1968) and his <u>Discourse on Inequality</u> (Kessinger, 2004).
11. Thomas Berry, <u>The Great Story</u> video (Bullfrog Films, 2002).

12. Sigmund Freud, <u>Civilization and its Discontents</u> (Norton, 1989).
13. John Stuart Mill, <u>Utilitarianism</u> (Penguin Classics, 1975) and <u>On Liberty</u> (Penguin Classics, 1975).
14. Freud, <u>Civilization.</u>
15. Mircea Eliade, <u>The Sacred and the Profane</u> (Harper, 1961).
16. Wayne Teasdale, <u>The Mystic Heart</u> (New World, 1999).
17. Karl Marx, <u>Das Kapital: a Critique of Political Economy</u> (Gateway, 1965).
18. Phillip Daileader, <u>Early Middle Ages</u> lecture series (The Teaching Company).

19. H. Longon, Leonardo (Kindersly, 1928), tr. John Gilber, ed. Neil Lockley.
20. Henri Nouwen, Making all things New (Harper, 1981). He has an excellent discussion of this in his opening section, "All these other things".
21. J.R.R. Tolkien in his Lord of the Rings trilogy. Published by Ballantine Books, New York, as a set: The Hobbit, The Fellowship of the Ring, The Two Towers and The Return of the King (1993).
22. Joseph Campbell, The Hero with a Thousand Faces (Princeton, 1972).
23. Carl Jung, see his books Modern Man in Search of a Soul (Harvest, 1955) and The Undiscovered Self (Bollingen, 1990).
24. On Existentialism, see Robert Solomon's lecture series No Excuses: Existentialism and the Meaning of Life by The Teaching Company and Soren Kierkegaard, especially Fear and Trembling, Either/Or and Concluding Unscientific Postscript.
25. See Carl Jung, Man and His Symbols (Dell, 1964) and Joseph Campbell, The Power of Myth (Anchor, 1991).
26. Campbell, Hero.
27. Robert Moore, The Archetype of Initiation: Sacred Space, Ritual Process and Personal Transformation (Xlibris, 2001). I had the privilege of studying under Dr. Moore at Chicago Theological Seminary for my D. Min. This volume is a collection of essays and lectures building upon the work of Joseph Campbell, Mircea Eliade, Arnold van Gennep and Victor Turner. It is a scintillating sythesis.
28. M. L. McLure and C. L. Feltoe, The Pilgrimage of Etheria (S.P.C.K. 1919).
29. John Climacus, The Ladder of Divine Ascent (Paulist Press, 1982).
30. McLure, Etheria.
31. Simon Coleman and John Elsner, Pilgrimage: Past and Resent in the World Religions. (Harvard, 1995).
32. Malcolm X, The Autobiography of Malcolm X. (Ballantine Books, 1987).
33. Coleman and Elsner, Pilgrimage, chapter six, "India."
34. Ibid., p. 141.
35. Ibid., chapter 7.
36. Ibid.

37. Gernot Condolini, Labyrinth: Walking toward the Center (Crossroad, 2003).
38. Newgrange information booklet from Bru na Boinne Visitor Centre. Newgrange is a United Nations Global Heritage site and predates the pyramids of Egypt.
39. My understanding of Celtic Spirituality is essentially as synthesis of all that I've read, primarily William John Fitzgerald's Seven Secrets of the Celtic Spirit: A Journey to the Soul of Ireland (Thomas More, 2001), Timothy Joyce, Celtic Christianity: A Sacred Tradition, a Vision of Hope (Orbis, 1998), Philip J. Newell, [his Listening to the Heartbeat of God: A Celtic Spirituality (Paulist, 1997) is the first book I recommend to new readers], John O'Donohue, Anam Cara: A Book of Celtic Wisdom (Harper, 1997) was quite popular and Esther de Waal's The Celtic Way of Prayer: The Recovery of the Religious Imagination (Doubleday, 1997) was the first text I read on the topic.
40. Ted Olsen, Christianity and the Celts (Intervarsity Press, 2003).
41. Des Lavelle, The Skellig Story: Ancient Monastic Outpost (O'Brien Press, 1976).
42. Timothy Joyce, Celtic Christianity pp. 46ff.
43. Thomas Cahill, How the Irish Saved Civilization (Doubleday, 1995).
44. Ibid.
45. DeWaal, Celtic Way of Prayer, p.2.
46. Philip Freeman, St. Patrick of Ireland. (Simon and Shuster, 2004).
47. John Skinner, ed. The Confession of Saint Patrick (Image Books, 1998). Also contains St. Patrick's "Letter to Coroticus", the only two documents known to have been written by St. Patrick, and both late in his life.
48. Ian Bradley, Columba: Pilgrim and Pentitent (Wild Goose Publications, 1996).
49. Cahill, Irish.
50. Ibid.
51. Mary Earle and Sylvia Maddox, Praying with the Celtic Saints. (St. Mary's Press, 2000).
52. Richard Woods, The Spirituality of the Celtic Saints. (Orbis, 2000), pp.56f and James Harpur, Sacred Tracks: 2000 years of Christian Pilgrimage. U. of California Press, 2002), pp. 155-157.

53. Sellner, Wisdom of the Celtic Saints. P. 162.
54. Philippe Gloaguen (ed.) Routard Ireland (Hachette, 2000), travel guide. P. 375f and Harpur, Sacred Tracks, pp.155-157.
55. Found on the internet, "The End of Europe's Middle Ages", c. 1997 U. of Calgary and New Advent Catholic Dictionary, volume ten, c. 2003.
56. Jean Paul Sartre, see his essay The Transcendence of the Ego (1937) or his lecture Existentialism is a Humanism (1946) or his much more developed Being and Nothingness (1943) or his novel Nausea (1938).
57. Don Richter, "The Moral Value of Sport" in The Cresset. v.61, #3 Lent, 1998. pp.6-11.
58. Robert Moore, Archetype of Initiation.
59. Attributed to Socrates by Plato in Dialogues, from Michael Sugrue's lecture series Plato, Socrates, and the Dialogues by The Teaching Company.
60. "Isaac Newton" articles from Wikipedia and Encarta websites.
61. www.brainyquote.com/quotes/authors/a/albert_einstein.html.
62. Jung, Modern Man.
63. Viktor Frankl, Man's Search for Meaning. (Pocket Books, 1997).
64. Jill Haak Adels. The Wisdom of the Saints. Barnes and Noble Books. New York. 2004. p.119.
65. The Rule of St. Benedict. Translated by Anthony C. Meisel and M. L. del Mastro. 1975. Image Books. New York. p.13.
66. Ibid. p.14ff.
67. Ibid. p.28ff.
68. Ibid. p.31-2.
69. Brother Lawrence. The Practice of the Presence of God. 1984. Paraclete Press. Orleans, Massachusetts.
70. Ibid., p.95.
71. Matthew Fox's Creation Spirituality (Harper, 1991) begins with a beautiful poem on creation, pp. 1-4. Brian Swimme in Hidden Heart of the Cosmos, Diarmuid O'Murchu in Quantum Theology and Thomas Berry in The Great Work also discuss this.
72. For information on Quantum science, see Jim al-Khalili's Quantum: A Guide for the Perplexed (Weidenfeld and Nicolson, 2003), Kenneth Ford's The Quantum World: Quantum Science for Everyone (Harvard, 2004), Brian Greene's The Elegant Universe (Norton, 1999) or Richard Wolfson's lecture series

Einstein's Revolution and the Quantum Revolution: Modern Physics for the non-Scientist from The Teaching Company.
73. Berry, The Great Work.
74. Brian Swimme, Hidden Heart of the Cosmos. "A Multiplicity of Centers" pp. 80ff.
75. Jim al-Khalili, Quantum. Pp. 12-23.
76. Beatrice Bruteau, God's Ecstacy: Creating a Selfl-Creating World.(Crossroad, 1997).
77. Moore, Initiation. Pp. 59ff.
78. From "Mending Wall" by Robert Frost, Complete Poems. (Holt, 1964).
79. Webster's New World Dictionary. (World, 1966) p. 721.
80. Martin Buber, I and Thou. (Scribners, 1958).
81. Anne Wilson Schaef, Living in Process: Basic Truths for Living the Path of the Soul. (Ballantine, 1999), especially pp. 3-20.
82. Benjamin B. Lahey, Psychology: an Introduction. (McGraw-Hill, 2003), especially chapter 3, "Biological Foundations of Behavior", pp. 56ff.
83. Ibid.
84. Carl Jung, Man and his Symbols. Pp. 41f on the collective unconscious.
85. John O'Donohue, Anam Cara and Eternal Echoes.
86. Mary Low. Celtic Christianity and Nature. p.127.
87. Timothy Joyce. Celtic Christianity. p.17.
88. Joyce, Celtic Christianity. Pp. 10, 25.
89. Peter Berresford Ellis, The Druids, (Eerdmans, 1994).
90. Cahill, Irish Saved Civilization.
91. Patrick, Confession.
92. Bradley, Columba.
93. O'Donohue, Anam Cara. Also de Waal, Celtic Prayer, pp. 133-138.
94. O'Donohue, Anam Cara.
95. Julian of Norwich, Revelations of Divine Love. (Image, 1977).
96. "The Way of the Pilgrim" found in A Treasury of Russian Spirituality edited by George P. Fedotov (Nordland, 1975).
97. Esther De Waal, The Celtic Way of Prayer. Image Books, New York. 1997. p.200.
98. Alexander Carmichael, Carmina Gadelica, p.241.
99. Ibid. p.244.
100. Ibid. p.248.

101. Ibid. p. 210.
102. Philip Newell. Celtic Prayers from Iona. Paulist Press. New York. 1997. p.28.
103. Ibid. p.52.
104. Kathy Galloway, The Pattern of our Days. Paulist Press. New York. 1999. p.122.
105. Ibid. p.127.
106. Ibid. p.158.
107. Ibid.
108. Ibid. p.159.
109. Ibid.
110. St. Richard of Chichester died in 1253 and was canonized in 1262. His shrine was a center for pilgrimage until it was destroyed in the 16th century. The full text of his prayer is:

"Thanks be to thee, O Lord Jesus Christ, for all the benefits which thou has given us; for all the pains and insults which thou has borne for us. O most merciful Redeemer, friend, and brother, may we know thee more clearly, love thee more dearly, and follow thee more nearly, for thine own sake. Amen." (the United Methodist Hymnal, United Methodist Publishing House, Nashville, 1993, #493) It was popularized in the song "Day by Day" in the musical Godspell.
111. Inspired by Ephesians 6:13-17.
112.   Psalm 34:8.

Annotated Bibliography

Adam, David. A Celtic Psaltery. SPCK. London. 2001.
A modern collection and translation drawn from throughout the Celtic world, arranged according to subject matter.

Agnes, Mother Mary (SOLI). Island Song. SPCK. London. 2001.
The author shares from her life as a solitary for 20 years on the remote island of Fetlar, in the Shetlands.

Aitchison, Nick. Macbeth: Man and Myth. Sutton Publishing Limited. Phoenix Mill Stroud Gloucestershire, England. 1999.
An historical biography of the real Macbeth, lawful king of Scotland for nearly two decades who ruled with firmness, fairness and generosity during a very turbulent time.

Artress, Lauren. Walking a Sacred Path: Rediscovering the Labyrinth as a Spiritual Tool. C. 1005. Penguin Putnam Books. New York City, New York.
Important in the ancient and the medieval world, the labyrinth has reemerged today as a metaphor for the spiritual journey and personal transformation. Artress draws upon her education and experience to open us to both the outer and the inner experience of the labyrinth.

Au, Wilkie and Noreen Cannon. Urgings of the Heart: A Spirituality of Integration. Paulist Press.
Drawing from a variety of religious traditions and psychological disciplines, this book helps develop personal awareness with a goal toward wholeness and transcendence.

Baxter, Colin and E. Mairi MacArthur. Iona. Colin Baxter Ltd., Grantown-on-Spey, Scotland. 1999.
A brief overview of the geological, sociological and spiritual history of the island of Iona, a center for Celtic Christian Spirituality; beautifully captured in photographs.

Bell, John L. Come all you People. GIA Publications, Chicago. 1994.
A collection of hymns, songs and canticles from the Iona Community.

Bolen, Jean Shinoda. <u>Goddesses in Every Woman</u>. Harper. San
  Fransisco. 2004
  <u>Gods in Everyman.</u> Harper. 1990.
  Jean Bolen is a Jungian analyst who studies of archetypal
  structures within the human subconsciousness.
Brown, Peter. <u>Augustine of Hippo: A Biography</u>.
  An account of one of the greatest minds in western Christianity,
  who nearly single handedly drove out Pelagius and Celtic
  spirituality from all acceptable thought and practice.
Bradley, Ian. <u>Columba: Pilgrim and Penitent</u>. Wild Goose
  Publications. Glasgow. 1996.
  This is a modern telling of the life of one of the most influential
  of all Celtic figures, perhaps second only to Patrick himself.
Brady, Ciaran, ed. <u>The Encyclopedia of Ireland</u>. Oxford University
  Press. Oxford. 2000.
  A compendium of people, places and events from Irish history,
  with several longer essays.
Bruteau, Beatrice. <u>God's Ecstasy: the Creation of a Self-Creating
  World.</u> Crossroad. New York. 1997.
  Bruteau brings her understanding of Teilhard de Chardin to the
  concept of the universe as an expression of God's ectasy and
  invites us into the process of Christogenesis, the growth of an
  ever greater Christ.
Cahill, Thomas. <u>Desire of the Everlasting Hills: The World Before
  and After Jesus</u>. Doubleday. New York. 1999.
  In a very readable narrative, we are presented with the historical
  Jesus and the world he lived in, and how his life has influenced
  all of history, for Christian and non-Christian alike.
Cahill, Thomas. <u>The Gifts of the Jews Anchor</u>. New York. 1999.
  In this volume, Cahill studies the view that history is
  progressive, as first presented by the Jews.
Cahill, Thomas. <u>How the Irish Saved Civilization: The Untold Story
  of Ireland's Heroic Role from the Fall of Rome to the Rise of
  Medieval Europe</u>. Doubleday. New York. 1995.
  In a popular book, the author introduces us to the world of the
  Celtic monks and the role they played in not only spreading
  Christianity, but even civilization itself after the collapse of the
  Roman Empire.

Cahill, Thomas. Sailing the Wine Dark Sea. Anchor. New York. 2004.
In this volume, Cahill presents the gift of philosophy we have inherited from the Greeks.

Cameron, Julia, with Mark Bryan. The Artist's Way: A Spiritual Path to Higher Creativity. Putnam. New York. 1992.
Designed as a personal workbook for a twelve week course in discovering and recovering the creative self, includes exercises, reflections and inspirational quotes.

Campbell, Joseph. The Hero with a Thousand Faces. Princeton University Press. Princeton, New Jersey. 1972.

Campbell, Joseph. The Power of Myth. Anchor. New York. 1991.
Originally a television interview with Bill Moyers, this presents Campbell's views and insights on myth in a conversational manner.

Carmichael, Alexander. Carmina Gadelica. Floris Books. Edinburg. 1994.
Alexander Carmichael spent his adult life scouring the highlands for these hymns and prayer that are both ancient and private. His collection and publication was seminal in the modern Celtic revival.

Clancy, Padgraigin. Celtic Threads: Exploring the Wisdom of our Heritage. Veritas Publications. Dublin. 1999.
This is a collection of some of the best essays by the most influential authors examining the influence and authenticity of modern Celtic spirituality.

Clift, Jean Dalby and Wallace B. The Archetype of Pilgrimage: Outer Action with Inner Meaning. Paulist Press. New York. 1996.
Jungian perspectives on religious and secular pilgrimages, toward developing a universal pattern in human experience. Geographic pilgrimage as acting out an inner journey.

Cloutgh, Juliet and Keith Davidson, Sandie Randall and Alastair Scott. Eyewitness Travel Guide to Scotland. DK Publishing, Inc. London. 1999.
An historical and contemporary introduction to Scotland for the traveler; includes historical, cultural and popular highlights.

Coleman, Simon & John Elsner. Pilgrimage: Past and Present in the World Religions. Connolly, S. J., ed. The Oxford Companion to Irish History. Oxford University Press. Oxford. 1998.
A one volume encyclopedia of people, places and events of importance in Irish history.

Condolini, Gernot. Labyrinth: Walking Toward the Center. Crossroad Publishing. New York. 2003.
The author offers the labyrinth as a map of the soul and a path of pilgrimage, by which we may be guided through the twists and turns of life.

Connolly, S. J. ed. The Oxford Companion to Irish History. Oxford University Press. Oxford. 1998.
A one volume encyclopedia of people, places and events of importance in Irish history.

Constable, Nick and Karen Farrington. Ireland. Barnes and Noble Books. New York. 1997.
A study of the land, history, arts and food of the Irish people.

Cousineau, Phil. The Art of Pilgrimage: Seeker's Guide to Making Travel Sacred. Conari Press. Berkeley California. 1998.
In this beautiful and poignantly written book, Cousineau offers perspectives on pilgrimage from around the world, plus his own insights.

Cousineau, Phil. The Soul of the World: A Modern Book of Hours. Harper. San Francisco. 1993.
Alternating pictures and quotes from around the world, we are given an inclusive and eclectic celebration of the sacredness of all life.

Cronin, Deborah. Holy Ground: Celtic Christian Spirituality. Upper Room Books. Nashville. 1999.
In a semi-autobiographical style, the author shares her insights from experience and research into Celtic spirituality, opening the reader up to reflection and insight.

Cronin, Michael. A History of Ireland. Palgrave Books. New York. 2001.
A succinct and illuminative account of a very complex and problematic history.

Cross, Tom P. and Clark Harris Slover (ed.). Ancient Irish Tales.
Barnes and Noble
Books. New York. 1996.
A reprint of a 1936 collection containing a wealth of tales from
ancient Ireland.
Cunliffe, Barry. The Ancient Celts. Oxford University Press. Oxford.
1997.
Through a careful study of all available information and
material, the author draws a thorough depiction of the history
and culture of the Celts and their lingering influence throughout
Europe.
The Dalai Lama and Howard C. Cutler, M.D. The Art of Happiness:
A Handbook for Living. Penguin Putnam. New York. 1998.
The purpose of life is to seek, experience and express happiness.
But what is happiness? Happiness is intimacy, connectivity and
compassion. This book offers helps for embarking on a
spirituality of happiness from the perspective of Tibetan
Buddhism.
Dames, Michael. Ireland: A Sacred Journey. Barnes and Noble
Books. New York. 2000.
A survey of Irish spirituality, including both pagan Celtic and
Christian influences; explores the interplay between myth and
history.
Davies, Oliver.   Celtic Spirituality. Paulist Press. Mahwah, N.J.
1999.
Part of the "Classics of Western Spirituality" series, this volume
is a very full introduction to the subject, offering a thorough
general introduction to the subject and a wealth of readings, each
with its own introduction.
Davies, Oliver and Fiona Bowie. Celtic Christian Spirituality: An
Anthology of Medieval and Modern Resources. Continuum.
New York. 1995.
A collection of ancient and vibrant writings from Celtic
spirituality that is both accessible and authoritative.
Donnelly, James S. Jr. The Great Irish Potato Famine. Sutton
Publishing. Gloucestershire. 2001.
A powerful account of one of the greatest tragedies of European
history, when a third of Ireland's population either died or
emigrated. Thoroughly analyzes all the causes and consequences
of this human catastrophe.

119

Dunphy, Madelin. The Peregrine's Journey. Millbrook.
A narration of the life cycle of he Peregrine falcon, complete with tales of its incredible flights.

Earle, Mary and Sylvia Maddox. Praying with the Celtic Saints. St. Mary's Press. Winona, Minnesota. 1997.
An introduction to Celtic spirituality through the lives of fifteen historic saints. Both practical and profound, it is an introduction that is personal and evocative, not just intellectual.

Eliade, Mircea. The Myth of the Eternal Return: Cosmos and History. Princeton University Press. Princeton, New Jersey. 1954.

Eliade, Mircea. The Sacred and the Profane: The Nature of Religion. Harper Torchbooks. New York. 1961.
The noted religious historian examines the total human experience to find the significance of religious myth, symbolism and ritual within life and culture.

Ellis, Peter Berresford. Celtic Myths and Legends. Carroll and Graf. New York.
A collection of classic tales from throughout the Celtic world that is interesting and inspring.

Ellis, Peter Berresford. The Druids. Eerdmans Publishing. Grand Rapids, Michigan. 1994.
A readable and reliable study by a respected author, sifting through available evidence to determine who the Druids were in Celtic society, their role, their training and their influence.

Evans, Robert F. Pelagius: Inquiries and Reappraisals. 1968. Seabury Press.New York.
Pelagius was a theologian of the 4th century who drew heavily on scripture and the nascent tradition of his time to argue for a positive understanding of the world and human potential. He was forced out by Augustine and his neo-platonism.

Ferguson, Ronald. Chasing the Wild Goose: The Story of the Iona Community. Wild Goose Publications. Glasgow. 1998.
Ronald Ferguson was leader of the Iona Community 1981-1988; the final chapter is by his successor, Norman Shanks. This is an inside view of the Iona Community, begun by St. Columba and renewed by Rev. George MacLeod.

Fitzgerald, William John. A Contemporary Celtic Prayer Book.
ACTA Publications. Chicago. 1998.
Offering prayers through the day, the week, the seasons and the
years, this collection invites us to discover the divine presence in
our daily lives.

Fitzgerald, William John. Seven Secrets of the Celtic Spirit: A
Journey to the Soul of Ireland. Thomas More. Allen, Texas.
2001.
Designed to be read reflectively, this volume looks at the core of
Celtic spirituality: trinity and circle, life as pilgrimage and as
dance, kinship with all things physical and spiritual, the sense of
wonder and humor. It is sprinkled liberally with stories, poetry
and insights.

Ford, Kenneth W. The Quantum World: Quantum Physics for
Everyone. Harvard University Press. Cambridge. 2004.
The former director of the American Institute of Physics offers
an introduction to quantum physics for the general reader.

Frankl, Victor. Man's Search for Meaning. Pocket Books. 1997.
Frankl shares his personal experience of being imprisoned in a
Nazi concentration camp, analyzes his survival and extrapolates
from it for our broader human experience.

Frankl, Victor.The Unconscious God: Psychotherapy and Theology.
Simon and Schuster. New York. 1975.
The founder of logotherapy explores the human significance of
our concept of God.

Frankl, Victor. The Unheard Cry for Meaning: Psychotherapy and
Humanism. Simon and Schuster. New York. 1978.
On the importance of helping people find meaning for their lives
so that they may live to their full potential as human beings.

Freeman, Philip. St. Patrick of Ireland.2004. Simon and Shuster. New
York.
This book attempts to get at the man behind the myth, the boy
from Britain who is transformed by years of slavery to a man
passionate for the Irish people.

Freud, Sigmund. Civilization and its Discontents. W.W. Norton &
Co. New York. 1989.
Freud argues that the demands of the civilization we have
created and our own innate needs are in conflict, and this leads to
stress and frustration in our lives, and the acting out of various
aggressive behaviors.

Fowler, James W. Becoming Adult, Becoming Christian: Adult Development and Christian Faith. Jossey-Bass Publishers. San Francisco. 2000.
Grounded in developmental psychology and theology, the author looks at maturation and selfhood and the struggle for identity and the spirituality of vocation.

Fowler, James W. Stages of Faith: The pscyhology of Human Development and the Quest for Meaning. Harper San Francisco. 1981.
Fowler's original work in human development and spiritual formation. An invaluable aid in our own quest for meaning and value.

Galloway, Kathy (ed.). The Pattern of our Days: Worship in the Celtic Tradition from the Iona Community. Paulist Press, Mahwah N.J. 1996.
Offers a wealth of worship material and inspiration that has been created and tested by the Iona community off the coast of Scotland.

Geoffrion, Jill Kimberly Hartwell. Praying the Labyrinth: A Journal for Spiritual Exploration. 1999. Pilgrim Press. Cleveland, O.
A personal journal with scripture, questions and poetry, to be used as spiritual exercises for personal reflection with the labyrinth.

Geoffrion, Jill Kimberly Hartwell and Elizabeth Catherine Nagel. The Labyrinth and the Enneagram: Circling into Prayer. 2001. Pilgrim Press.   Cleveland, O.
This workbook combines two popular approaches in spiritual formationto help the pilgrim-participant grow toward a deeper connection with the sacred.

Gulley, Phillip. For Everything a Season: Simple Musings on Living Well. Multnomah Press. Sisters, Oregon. 1999.
Humorous, homespun stories, gentle and wise, reminding us that the moment we are born, we embark on a journey through the seasons of life. The book illuminates the truth of Ecclesiastes 3:1-8.

Haining, Peter. Great Irish Humor. Barnes and Noble Books. New York. 1996.
A collection of thirty five short stories proving that nothing in all Ireland or Irish history is beyond the reach of Irish humor.

Harpur, James. Sacred Tracks: 2000 years of Christian Pilgrimage. University of California Press. 2002. The author traces the history of Christian pilgrimage from its beginnings to the modern era and with a variety of destinations.

Harris, Nathaniel. Heritage of Scotland: A Cultural History of Scotland and its People. Checkmark Books. London. 2000. A study of the major events of Scottish history, the people who figured in them and the people affected by them.

Hays, Edward. Prayers for a Planetary Pilgrim: A Personal Manual for Prayer and Ritual. 1989. Forest of Peace Publishing. Leavenworth, Kansas. Designed to help those who see their lives as a sacred journey, this book speaks of a spirituality that keeps pace with the scientific and technological developments of our time.

Haywood, John. Atlas of the Celtic World. Thames and Hudson. London. 2000. An historical atlas of the Celtic people and culture, from pre-history to the current day.

Henry, Patrick. The Ironic Christian's Companion: Finding the Marks of God's Grace in the World. 1999. Penguin Putnam. New York. Written with wit and humor, this book tells stories that waken the imagination and help us enjoy the journey that our lives are on.

Hogue, David. Remembering the Future, Imagining the Past: Story, Ritual and the Human Brain. Pilgrim Press. Cleveland. 2003. A discussion between theology and brain science, reshaping how we understand imagination, memory and experience, shaping our future and reshaping our past.

Huisinga, Johan. Homo Ludens: A Study of the Play Element in Culture. Beacon Press. Boston. 1955. A seminal work by the sociologist arguing that we are not just "homo sapiens" or "homo faber", people thinking and making, but also "homo ludens", people at play, and the concept of play is an important part of our culture and our civilization.

Huston, Paula. The Holy Way: Practices for a Simple Life. Loyola Press. Chicago. 2003. The author studies the lives of hermits and monks and of contemporary religious and applies those lessons in spirituality and simplicity to her own life.

The Iona Community. <u>Iona Abbey Worship Book.</u> Wild Goose Publications. Glasgow. 2001.
A collection of a variety of services and resources used by the Iona Community

Johnson, Ben Campell. <u>Listening for God: Spiritual Directives for Searching Christians.</u>1997. Paulist Press. Mahwah, New Jersey. Re-writing the Spiritual Exercises of St. Ignatius for the contemporary mind and an ecumenical setting.

Johnson, Robert. <u>He: Understanding Masculine Psychology</u> (1989) <u>She: Understanding Feminine Psychology</u> (1989) <u>We: Understanding the Psychology of Romantic Love</u> (1983) <u>Ecstasy: Understanding the Psychology of Joy</u> (1989) <u>Owning your Own Shadow: Understanding the Dark Side of the Psyche</u> (1991) <u>The Fisher King and the Handless Maiden</u> (1993) Robert Johnson is a Jungian analyst, lecturer and author.

Jones, Gwyn and Trevor Jones, ed. <u>The Mabinogion.</u> Alfred A. Knopf. New York. 1993.
This is a modern translation of a fourteenth century collection of ancient Welsh legends offering illumination to the Celtic imagination, their approach to life as journey and adventure, and containing some seeds for the later development of the Arthurian cycle.

Jones, John Miriam. <u>With an Eagle's Eye: Seven Day Sojourn in Celtic Spirituality.</u> Ave Marie Press. Notre Dame, Indiana. 1998. Designed to be used as a personal retreat experience in Celtic Spirituality, this book emphasizes key points of the Celtic experience: the immanent presence of the divine in all things, the dynamic tension between the personal and the community, the expressiveness of the faith, faith as a lived journey and the necessity of commitment.

Josse, Pierre, chief editor. <u>Ireland.</u> Hachette Press. London. 2000. The Routard guide for travelers. A careful and detailed guide with information and background for touring throughout Ireland.

Joyce, Timothy. <u>Celtic Christianity: A Sacred Tradition, A Vision of Hope.</u> Orbis Books. Maryknoll, New York. 1998.
Celtic spirituality appeals to the whole person, mind, body and soul, and the whole of life. This book invites us to see the heroic in the everyday and the miraculous in the mundane.

Jung, Carl. Man and His Symbols. Dell Publishing. New York. 1964.
Jung's last written work prior to his death, a culmination of his life's work written in non-technical terms.

Jung, Carl. Modern Man in Search for a Soul. Harvest Books. New York. 1955.
A wide ranging consideration of the spiritual and psychological issues of modern times.

Jung, Carl. Psychology and Religion. Yale University Press. New Haven. 1960.
A series of lectures given on each topic and their juxtaposition in human experience.

Jung, Carl. The Undiscovered Self. Bollingen. 1990.
The importance of self discovery and self knowledge. Either we discover who we are or we lose who we are.

Kabat-Zinn, Jon. Wherever you Go, There you are: Mindfulness Meditation in Everyday Life. Hyperion. New York. 1994.
A Zen Buddhist writes about being fully present in the present moment and living life as a meditative state.

Al-Khalili, Jim. Quantum: a Guide for the Perplexed. Weidenfeld and Nicolson. London. 2003.
A theoretical physicist and lecturer offers this informative and entertaining introduction to quantum theory.

Keneally, Thomas. The Great Shame: and the Triumph of the Irish in the English Speaking World. Doubleday. New York. 1998.
The author of Schindler's List recounts with great detail and personal impact the struggle of the Irish to maintain their cultural and national identity. A grand epic tale.

Kushner, Harold S. Living a Life that Matters: Resolving the Conflict between Conscience and Success. Knopf. New York. 2001.
The renowned author and rabbi suggests we live a life based upon integrity, flowing from who we are and who we want to be.

Ladinsky, Daniel, tr. The Gift: Poems by Hafiz. Penguin Compass. New York. 1999.
A comprehensive collection of contemporary translations from the great Sufi master, offering a view of Islam rarely seen in the west: playful, wondrous and profound.

125

Lavelle, Des. The Skellig Story: Ancient Monastic Outpost. O'Brien
Press. Dublin. 1976.
The Skelligs were for the Irish what Mt. Athos was for the
Greeks. These harsh islands were a spiritual haven from the 5th to
the 12th centuries.

Levine, Stephen. A Gradual Awakening. Anchor Press. Garden City,
New Jersey. 1979.
The author is a teacher and practitioner of Buddhist vipassana
meditation. This book is about awareness, mindfulness and
simplicity, for those who realize life is a journey and are ready to
begin.

Lonegren, Sig. Labyrinths: Ancient Myths and Modern Uses. Sterling
Publishing. New York. 1996.
A study that draws heavily on ancient uses of the labyrinth,
includes non-Western use, and only secondarily Christian
influence, thereby offering a unique perspective. Includes guided
exercises for personal use.

Low, Masry. Celtic Christianity and Nature. Edinburgh University
Press. Edinburgh. 1996.
Low pushes herself as a historian to avoid sentimentalism in this
study of pre-Christian and Christian Celtic understandings of
nature and the world around them.

Mackay, James. William Wallace: Brave Heart. Mainstream
Publishing. Edinburgh. 1995.
A search for the historical figure of Wallace; who he was, how
he lived, what he did, and how he influenced the Scottish psyche.

MacLean, Fitzroy. Highlanders: A History of the Scottish Clans.
Penguin Studio Books. New York. 1995.
A study of the history and development of the Highland clans,
from the invasion of the Scotti of the Irish kingdom of Dalriada
to the clearings and cultural revivals of the 19th century.

MacMullen, Ramsay.   Christianity and Paganism in the Fourth to
Eighth Centuries. Yale University Press. New Haven. 1997.
Covering a critical period for Celtic spirituality and writing from
the perspective of the continental experience, this book argues
that Christianity spread by assimilation, not obliteration.

MacNab, P. A. Mull and Iona. Pevensey Press. Brunel House, Newton Abbot, Devon, England. 1995.
The history, geology, biology and mythology of the twin islands of Mull and Iona, off the western coast of Scotland. Filled with interesting anecdotes and beautiful photographs, includes references for further reading.

Marsden, John. The Tombs of the Kings: An Iona Book of the Dead. Llanerch Publishers. Felinfach. 1994.
Iona is an island holy to Scotland and to Celtic spirituality. Over the centuries, dozens of rulers from the realms of Celtic influence were buried here. This book introduces us to the Reilig Odhrain, the burial ground of kings, that is on Iona.

Mathers, Ewan. The Cloisters of Iona Abbey. Wild Goose Publications. Glasgow. 2001.
The Abbey is the spiritual center for the holy island of Iona, and the heart of the Abbey is as much the cloister as the chapel. This volume is a photographic essay that captures the spirit of the place.

Matthews, Caitlin. The Celtic Tradition. Element Books. Rockport, Mass. 1995.
An exploration of all the pagan and non-Christian influences of Celtic culture, and the Celtic influence upon contemporary culture.

Matthews, Caitlin and John. The Encyclopedia of Celtic Wisdom: A Celtic Shaman's Sourcebook. Element Books. Rockport, Mass. 1994.
This volume collects myths, stories and legends from the pre-Christian Celts and arranges them by subject matter. An insightful look at an ancient culture.

McCourt, Frank. Angela's Ashes: A Memoir. Scribner. New York. 1996.
A Pulitzer Prize winning autobiography of growing up in Ireland during the Depression.

McCourt, Malachy. Malacy McCourt's History of Ireland. Running Press. Philadelphia. 2004.
The highly acclaimed author and actor writes an engaging history of his beloved land; history made personable.

McCourt, Malachy. Voices of Ireland: Classic Writings of a Rich and Rare Land. Running Press. Philadephia. 2002.
A thick and rich collection of some of the best of Irish writing, from Jonathon Swift to Michael Collins.

McCullough, David Willis. Wars of the Irish Kings. History Book Club. New York. 2000.
An anthology of a thousand years of internal warfare, from the age of myths to the time of Elizabeth.

McLure, M. L. & C. L. Feltoe. The Pilgrimage of Etheria. S.P.C.K. London. 1919.
A translation of the journal kept by Etheria, a 4th century nun who traveled from Spain to Jerusalem.

McMahon, James M. The Price of Wisdom: The Heroic Struggle to Become a Person. 1996. Crossroad Publishing. New York.
The author draws from his twenty-five years of experience in psychology for insight on being a whole, mature, actualized human being, spiritually as well as psychologically.

Mead, Margaret. And Keep your Powder Dry: An Anthropologist Looks at America. Berghahn Books. 2000.
The famous anthropologist looks at her native land and culture. A classic work on a par with de Tocqueville.

Mead, Margaret. The Study of Culture at a Distance. Berghahn Books. 200.
How to understand different cultures through their film and literature, interviews and focus groups. Explores diverse cultures through these methods.

Meehan, Bridget Mary & Regina Madonna Oliver. Praying with Celtic Holy Women.
Based upon the authors' personal research and experiences in Ireland and Wales, this is an excellent introduction to Celtic spirituality as a whole and to the amazing influence of women within this tradition.

Miller, Whitney G. Psychomysticism: Toward a Method of Contemplative Counseling. Gradutate Theological Foundation. Donaldson, Indiana. 1997.
The author is trained in theology and psychology and personally inspired by the work of Bernard Lonergan. This book is a study of these influences, seeking for therapeutic convergence. It encourages us to be attentive, authentic, reasonable and responsive to find compassion for ourselves and others.

Moore, Robert L. The Archetype of Initiation: Sacred Space, Ritual Process, and Personal Transformation. Xlibris Corporation. Chicago. 2001.
The noted psychoanalyst and professor combines insights from contemporary psychoanalytical theory with understandings from primitive tribal culture to describe life as a journey of transformation.

Moore, Robert L. Carl Jung and Christian Spirituality. Paulist Press. 1988.
A collection of essays on topics relating Jung to Christianity.

Moore, Robert L. Jung's Challenge to Contemporary Religion. Chiron Press. 1987.
A collection of essays on topics relating Jung to Christianity.

Moore, Robert L. King, Warrior, Magician, Lover: Rediscovering the Archetype of the Mature Masculine. Harper. San Francisco. 1991.
A Jungian introduction to the psychological foundations of a mature, authentic and revitalized masculinity, highlighting the differences between boy psychology and man psychology.

Morgan, John H. Being Human: Perspctives on Meaning and Interpretation, Essays in Religion, Culture and Personality. 2002. Quill Books. Bristol, Indiana.
This book examine's our human search for personal meaning from a wide range of disciplines and philosophies.

Morgan, John H. From Freud to Frankl: Our Modern Search for Personal Meaning.1987. Wyndham Hall Press.
An introduction to the search for meaning from the leading philosophers of modern western society.

Munro, Eleanor. On Glory Rloads: A Pilgrim's Book about Pilgrimage. Thames and Hudson. New York. 1987.
On the human urge to endow life with meaning. From our primitive past to medieval and modern pilgrimages, religious and secular. Looks at Mecca, Graceland and Australian "walkabouts", on being and becoming.

Newell, Philip J. Celtic Prayers from Iona. Paulist Press. New York. 1997.
A wonderful little daily devotional filled with inspiration from Iona.

Newell, Philip J. The Book of Creation: An Introduction to Celtic
Spirituality. Paulist Press. New York. 1999.
In this volume the author introduces us to Celtic spirituality
through the seven days of creation from Genesis 2.

Newell, Philip J. Listening for the Heartbeat of God: A Celtic
Spirituality. Paulist Press. Mahwah, N. J. 1997.
A wonderful, simple, profound introduction to Celtic spirituality.
Perhaps the best "first book" to read on the subject.

Newell, Philip J. One Foot in Eden: A Celtic View of the Stages of
Life. Paulist Press. Mahwah, N.J. 1999.
A reflection of human life stages from a perspective of Celtic
spirituality that invites us to see our own life as a journey of
discovery.

Newton, Michael. A Handbook of the Scottish Gaelic World. Four
Courts Press. Portland, Oregon. 2000.
While Romanized Europe on the continent underwent the Dark
Ages, the Celtic world of the islands experienced their Heroic
Age. This book looks at the Heroic Age in Scotland, principally
the 8th through 16th centuries.

Norwich, Juliana of. Revelations of Divine Love. Image Books.
Garden City, New York. 1977.
A 14th century solitary records her twenty year dialogue with a
most personal God. In spite of plague, fever, homelessness, and
the uncertainties of her life, she can say, "All will be well and all
will be well and all manner of things will be well."

O'Donohue, John. Anam Cara: A Book of Celtic Wisdom. Harper
Collins. 1997.
"Anam Cara" is Gaelic for "Soul Friend" and this book attempts
to be just that. Drawing from the full scope of Celtic spirituality,
both Christian and pre-Christian, the author examines the full
range of human experience.

O'Donohue, John. Eternal Echoes: Celtic Reflections on our
Yearning to Belong.1999. Harper Collins. New York.
Seeing our inner restlessness as an expression of the divine
within us, this book explores our desire to belong as that which
gives us the energy for self-discovery and creativity and the
courage to risk friendship.

Olsen, Ted. Christianity and the Celts. Intervarsity Press. Downers Grove. IL. 2003.
This is a very readable and concise introduction that manages to maintain its own perspective as it moves through the Celtic world.

O'Murchu, Diarmuid. Religion in Exile: A Spiritual Homecoming. Crossroad Books. New York. 2000.
Using the mythic symbolism of exile and return, the author offers of contemporary revisioning of spirituality for the journey.

O'Se', Diarmuid and Joseph Sheils. Teach Yourself Irish (books and tapes). NTC Publishing. Lincolnwood Illinois. 1993.
A complete introductory course for reading and speaking Irish Gaelic.

Osborne-McKnight, Juilene. I am of Irelaunde: A Novel of Patrick and Osian. 2000. Forge Books. New York.
In novel form, this book uses the stories of Patrick and Osian to waken our own imagination for our spiritual life journeys.

St. Patrick. Confessions and Letter to Coraticus.
The only written documents we have from the hand of the best known Celtic saint. Patrick makes a humble and impassioned declaration of his life and faith.

Pearson, Carol S. Awakening the Heroes Within: Twelve Archetypes to help us find ourselves and transform our world. Harper. San Francisco. 1991.
Describes the heroic quest as one of self discovery, becoming more fully alive and effective. Writing about soul and soul development and written for people who want to realize their full potential.

Pennick, Nigel. The Celtic Saints: An Illustrated and Authoritative Guide to these Extraordinary Men and Women. Sterling Publishing. New York. 1997.
An entrance to the Celtic world through legends, myths and stories of the key figures of Celtic history.

Pilgrim, Peace. Peace Pilgrim: Her Life and Work in her own Words. Ocean Tree. Sanata Monica, CA. 1994.
Peace Pilgrim was an anonymous woman who walked throughout America with a message of personal and societal peace.

Ramshaw, Gail. A Metaphorical God: An Abecedary of Images for
    God. 1995. Liturgy Training Publications. Chicago, Illinois.
    According to one legend, God's first creation was the alphabet,
    from which God created everything else. This book uses the
    alphabet to present different modern metaphors for the image of
    God in our own lives.
Rees, Elizabeth. Celtic Saints: Passionate Wanderers. 2000. Thames
    and Hudson. New York.
    This book tells the stories of a number of Celtic saints,
    describing them as wanderers on a passionate pilgrimage.
Rohr, Richard, and Joseph Martos. The Wild Man's Journey:
    Reflections on Male Spirituality. St. Anthony Messenger Press.
    Cincinnati.
    This is a collection of writings and teachings by Richard Rohr on
    issues of male spirituality, edited by Joseph Martos.
Rupp, Joyce. May I Have This Dance? Ave Maria Press. Notre Dame
    Indiana. 2001.
    An invitation to join with God in the dance of life through its
    daily and seasonal rhythms.
Rupp, Joyce. Walk in a Relaxed Manner: Life Lessons from the
    Camino. Orbis. Maryknoll. 2005.
    The author shares general lessons from her personal 37 day
    pilgrimage along the Camino de Santiago in Spain.
Sanders, Scott Russell. Staying Put: Making a Home in a Restless
    World. Beacon Press. 1994.
    Examines the consequences of displacement in our increasingly
    mobile society. The value of staying put, putting down roots,
    building community and memory, for personal formation.
Sands, Helen Raphael. The Healing Labyrinth: Finding your path to
    inner peace. Barron's. Hauppauge, New York. 2001.
    In our world of chaos and confusion, this book invites us on a
    meditative journey, drawing on dance, music and story-telling, to
    help us find the center of our own lives.
Schaef, Anne Wilson. Living in Process: Basic Truths for Living the
    Path of the Soul. Ballantine Books. New York. 1999.
    Everything, our lives, the world around us, the universe, is in
    process. Even process is in process. Living in process is a matter
    of living fully, deeply, participatively, honestly.

Scott, Ronald McNair. Robert the Bruce: King of Scots. Peter
Bedrick Books. New York. 1989.
Biography of one of the greatest kings of Scotland, crowned at
Scone in 1306, victor at Bannockburn in 1314, ruled until his
death in 1329.
Sellner, Edward C. Wisdom of the Celtic Saints. Ave Maria Press,
Notre Dame Indiana. 1993.
This volume begins with a thorough introduction to Celtic
spirituality, its overall themes and unique emphases, and then
moves through brief introductions to a panoply of Celtic saints.
Shanks, Norman. Iona: God's Energy; the Spirituality and Vision of
the Iona Community. Hodder & Stoughton. London. 1999.
The tiny island of Iona has been regarded a "thin place" from the
dawn of time and today draws 120,000 visitors daily. This book
looks at the experience and the spirituality of the contemporary
Iona Community.
Sheldrake, Philip. Living Between Worlds: Place and Journey in
Celtic Spirituality. Crowley Publications. 1995.
The impact of traditional Celtic beliefs on Christian worship and
the role of liminality.
Simpson, Ray. Celtic Blessings: Prayers for Everyday Life. Loyola
Press, Chicago. 1999.
Both spiritual and practical, this book contains blessings for
everyday events, formal occasions, daily and seasonal rituals and
key steps in life's journeys. It is written with the felt knowledge
that life is indeed a pilgrimage.
Spadaro, Katherine and Katie Graham. Colloquial Scottish Gaelic
(book and tapes). Routledge Press. New York. 2001.
A complete course in colloquial Scots Gaelic, in written and
spoken form.
Sumption, Jonathon. The Age of Pilgrimage: The Medieval Journey
to God. 2003. Paulist Press. Mahwah, New Jersey.
Writing with both sympathy and passion, this book describes the
world of the medieval pilgrimage, their view of the world and
view of the self.
Sykes, Homer. Celtic Britain. Cassell and Company. London. 2001.
Drawing from landscapes and artifacts, this is a pictorial essay
the evokes the spirit of the Celtic people and culture.

Tanner, Marcus. The Last of the Celts. Yale University Press. New Haven. 2004
The author shares his journey through the Celtic world to find that, despite the popularity of all things "Celtic", genuine Celtic culture is not only declining, but dying.

The Teaching Company. Chantilly VA.
Daileader, Philip. Early Middle Ages.
Pollock, Steven. Particle Physics for the Non-Physicist: A Tour of the Microcosmos.
Solomon, Robert. No Excuses: Existentialism and the Meaning of Life.
Sugrue, Michael. Plato, Socrates and the Dialogues.
Tyson, Neil de Grasse. My Favorite Universe.
Wolfson, Richard. Einstein's Relativity and the Quantum Revolution: Quantum Physics for the non-Scientist.
These are taped lectures given by college professors who are noted in their fields of expertise. They offer a great way to exercise the brain while walking, exercising or driving.

St. Theophan the Recluse. The Path to Salvation: A Maual of Spiritual Transrformation. St. Herman of Alaska Brotherhood. St. Paisius Abbey. Forestville, California. 1996.
A masterpiece from the Hessycist tradition of Russian Orthodoxy, this book is a personal and detailed account of how to find the Kingdom of God within and dwell in the Grace of God.

Thompson, E. A. Who was St. Patrick? The Boydell Press. Woodbridge, Suffolk, England. 1999.
A careful examination through all the legend attached to Patrick to ascertain what may reasonably be established historically. Readable and reliable.

Torrance, Robert M. The Spiritual Quest: Transcendence in Myth, Relgion and Science. University of California Press. Berkely. 1994.
The quest as a dimension of human experience, humans as questing qanimals. Desire for transcendence as a form of quest experience and the experience of transcendence as a part of the quest.

Turner, Victor. Process, Performance and Pilgrimage: A Study in Comparative Symbology. Concept Publishing. New Delhi. 1979.

Turner, Victor. The Ritual Process: Structure and Anti-Structure. Aldine de Gruyter. Hawthorne, New York. 1995. A seminal analysis of ritual behavior and symbolism, introducing notions of "liminality" and "communitas". An anthropological study of the role of ritual in human culture and life.

Van de Weyer, Robert. Celtic Prayers: a Book of Celtic Devotion. Abingdon Press. Nashville. 1997 As we search for meaning in our lives, the ancient Celts can guide and inspire us. They found divine presence and purpose in every aspect of existence and the mundane chores of their everyday lives became encounters with the divine.

Vescoli, Michael. The Celtic Tree Calendar: Your Tree Sign and You. Souvenir Press. London. 1999. The ancient Celts respected and revered trees as living beings symbolizing the threefold cycle of life, death and rebirth. This book offers a horoscope based upon the guardian tree for each astrological season of the year.

Waal, Esther de. The Celtic Way of Prayer: The Recovery of the Religious Imagination. Doubleday. New York. 1997. Esther de Waal is one of Celtic spirituality's foremost scholars. This is an invigorating book that leads the reader into a full experience of the Celtic imagination in a way that frees us from formalism and is liberating as well as illuminating.

Waal, Esther de. The Celtic Vision: Prayers, Blessings, Songs and Invocations from the Gaelic Tradition. Ligouri Publications. Ligouri, Mo. 2001. The author's selection of favorites from Alexander Carmichael's massive Carmina Gadelica collection. A fine introduction

Walsh, James (tr.). The Cloud of Unknowing. Paulist Press. New York. 1981. A medieval classic of the mystical way, written by an anonymous 14th century English monk. This book offers a method of contemplation that stresses the inability of understanding to reach the divine, "it is love alone that can reach God."

Walsh, James (tr.). The Pursuit of Wisdom and Other Works. Paulist Press. New York. 1988.
Containing additional works by the anonymous author of The Cloud , stressing that technique is subservient to the burning love for the indwelling presence, which inspires us to active service on behalf of others.

Wessels, Cletus. The Holy Web: Church and the New Universe Story. Orbis Books. Maryknoll, New York. 2000.
A Dominican friar and former Theology professor calls for a new form of church and a new story of faith, based upon a dynamic "web of relationships" and drawing from the writings of Thomas Berry and Brian Swimme.

Westbury, Virginia. Labyrinths: Ancient paths of wisdom and peace. Lansdowne Publishing. Sydney. 2001.
A look at the uses and role of the labyrinth throughout human history for spirituality, meditation and peace. Includes a discussion of labyrinth design.

Whitehead, Evelyn Eaton and James D. Christian Life Patterns: The Psychological Challenges and Religious Invitations of Adult Life. Crossroad. New York. 2001.
Psychological patterns and changes in the human maturation process and their potential for spiritual creativity and fulfillment.

Wild Goose Worship Group. A Wee Worship Book. GIA Publications. Chicago. 1999.
A smaller collection of worship services and resources from the Iona Community.

Williamson, Duncan. Tales of the Seal People: Scottish Folk Tales. Interlink Books. New York. 1992.
The seal plays an important part in Celtic culture. Both the Irish and the Scottish have tales of seals and silkies, half seal and half human. This volume contains a collection of Scottish tales.

Wolfson, Margaret Olivia. The Turtle Tattoo: Timeless Tales for Finding and Fulfilling your Dreams. Nataraj Publishing. Mill Valley, California. 1996.
The author is a professional storyteller and uses folk tales and fairy tales to illuminate the treasures hidden around and within us and inspire us to find our own life's purpose.

Wood, Juliette. The Celtic Book of Living and Dying: An Illustrated Guide to Celtic Wisdom. 2000. Chronicle Books. San Francisco. Drawing on the treasury of Celtic folklore, this book shares stories inspired by everyday events and the ordinariness of life to find meaning and purpose for our lives.

Woods, Richard J. The Spirituality of the Celtic Saints. Orbis Books. Maryknoll, New York. 2000. Avoiding sentimentality, the author explores Celtic spirituality to find its relevance today, more politically charged than others.

Woods, Richard J. Insight Guide to Scotland. Insight Guides. London. 1999. A travel guide offering historical, geographical and cultural overviews and detailed introductions to the people and places of modern Scotland.